SABBATICAL OF THE MIND
The Journey from Anxiety to Peace

David L. Winters

Carpenter's Son Publishing

Published by **DAVIWIN** in cooperation with
Carpenter's Son Publishing Franklin, TN

Print ISBN-13: 978-0-9977747-0-2
ebook ISBN-13: 978-0-9977747-1-9

Cover Design: JD&J Design, LLC
Interior Design: Gary Jenkins

Printed in the U.S.A.

Scripture quotations: Holy Bible, King James Version, 1611.

For additional information please visit **sabbatical of the mind.net**.

Contents

FOREWORD

Sabbatical of the Mind is a perfect book for these fast-paced times in which we all live. Dave Winters's story takes readers on a humorous trip from extreme stress to serenity while providing interesting twists and turns along the way.

Dave is a genuine DC inside-the-Beltway success, having risen through the ranks as a civilian with the US Navy and a division director with a certain three-letter government agency. His awards and medals only partially attest to his many accomplishments in business and government service. As with many people, however, the price for his success came at the expense of unwanted pounds and related health problems. That is how Dave and I met.

As the pastor of Capital Baptist Church in the Washington DC suburb of Annandale, Virginia, I started the Losing to Live weight-loss program out of my desire to lose a significant amount of weight by honoring God with my body and through small, incremental lifestyle changes. Today Losing to Live has grown into a program that is now used in hundreds of churches in many denominations across America. I learned, and the program teaches, that we can enhance our witness for God and be more effective serving other people if we get our physical bodies into better shape.

David first heard a presentation about Losing to Live at a Christian conference sponsored by the Iron Sharpens Iron network. Since then he has participated in the weight-loss program at our church, first as a member of a team and eventually as a team captain. He has personally lost sixty pounds.

But losing weight was only part of Dave's journey. Like so many other people in our busy metropolitan area and throughout the world, the pressures of daily life left him little time for addressing life's big questions. Commuting to work, participating in volunteer activities, and taking care of family consumed all his free time. After brushes with a few serious medical issues, God gave him the foresight to realize that he needed more than just a few minutes of daily devotions or a weekend conference. Dave grew to want substantial life change, and he was willing to invest in it. Eventually God led him to the biblical concept of a sabbatical, which proved to be a potent prescription to remedy several of his issues. In his story he tells of exploring deep fears, learning to relax, and finding a new level of trust in God.

Dave's personal journey is relatable to anyone who has experienced fear and doubt in their lives and, at times, even in their faith. Like many people, Dave's journey from childhood involvement in a mainline-denomination church to falling away from God in young adulthood to eventually finding his way back to church will lead the reader to a closer, more personal relationship with God.

Though at times difficult and painful, such a spiritual journey leads to personal growth and a stronger faith.

Dave now regularly attends Capital Baptist Church and actively participates in many of our volunteer and outreach activities. He is a treasured member of our church family. Dave is a unique character with a unique perspective on some of the big questions of life we all must face.

I hope you enjoy the story of his sabbatical of the mind. As you read it, also respond to the invitation of Jesus, who said, "Come unto me, all ye that labour and are heavy laden, and I will give you rest" (Matt. 11:28).

Steve Reynolds

Pastor of Capital Baptist Church, Annandale, VA
Author of *Bod 4 God: The Four Keys to Weight Loss*
Creator of the Losing to Live weight-loss competition

ACKNOWLEDGMENTS

This book would not have been possible without several friends, relatives, book lovers, and a parrot named Bruno. Thank you to my test readers, advisers, and friends: noted author Elaine Biech, her husband, Dan, my sister, Susan Fouty, my niece, Laura Fouty Asher, Eric Bardin, John Folker, Gary Jenkins, and Eileen Powers. Without them none of this would have been so fun. Thanks also to a marvelous editor, Rebecca English. Most importantly, thank You to the one true God of us all. He is the great I Am, and it truly is all about Him. He has been so good to me for so long. I truly cannot complain.

Dedicated to the one true Savior of mankind, Jesus Christ

COMING TO THE END
OF MY ROPE

1

TRAFFIC WAS AS BAD AS EVER. My mood couldn't have been worse as I snaked my way west out of our nation's capital toward the Virginia suburbs.

After a hectic day at the three-letter government agency where I worked, I was not looking forward to another painful elders' meeting at church. Our small nondenominational congregation was dwindling in numbers and enthusiasm. Through a series of goofs, infidelities, and bad reactions, the brethren (and sisters) had thinned from almost 250 to 65 attending on Sunday mornings. This was a problem on many levels, most of them practical and financial. We just didn't have critical mass to do most of what we had done before. Our leadership team was feeling the heat, including its newest member—me.

Cars crept along K Street more slowly than legislation through a divided Congress. Suddenly a self-absorbed yuppie decided that his expensive Lexus or BMW or Infinity allowed him infinite lane changes. His large car payment obviously bought him the right to get to his yoga session ahead of the little people who wanted to see their children's Little League games or attend annoying church meetings.

When frustrated, I tended to get a little sarcastic. To lighten my mood, I imagined other drivers as one form of dog or another—sort of as in the Dogs Playing Poker artwork. The drivers who acted up were poodles and Chihuahuas. "Come on, puppy, you can do it," I said to a driver forcing his way into the lane ahead of me. "Make your move. Good boy. You did it!" While admittedly immature, I saw no harm in indulging myself in this area. It let me blow off steam without incident—usually.

Today as I drove to the elders' meeting, the stress was eating me up. I'd been delayed at work later than usual. I didn't want to go to the meeting hungry, but I was already going to be late.

I didn't like being late. Growing up, my mom had always set our family's clocks five to ten minutes fast so we would always be on time. We had been prompt scouts, baseball players, tennis players, church members, and volunteers. Thinking of my mom and traveling at the speed of slime, I decided to multitask. I punched Mom's number on my cell phone. She lived in the same small town where we had lived when I was growing up, about thirty miles from Dayton, Ohio. It's great in Dayton, I thought as the phone rang.

My late-eighty-something mom, a spry, happy, outspoken depression-surviving giver, was usually a great source of inspiration and laughter. Not this day. Today she was peeved at some friends who had apparently bickered past my Mom's too-much-bickering indicator. Mom gave me the play-by-play details. "Oh, the way they yell at each other. 'You do it.' 'No, you do it.' I could have had it cleaned up and driven home in the time they took to argue about it." She went on and on. On another day I would have said, "What else is new?" but today each word gnawed deeper and deeper into my brain. It was as if a knife were hacking small pieces from my cerebral cortex.

Finally I couldn't listen to another word. I started to cry into the phone. A forty-something, six-foot-tall, 270-pound man without shame, my sobs became louder and louder until Mom finally heard me. Instantly her demeanor changed. "What's the matter, sweetie?"

"Mom, I can't stand it anymore. I can't listen to this right now." Then fear gripped me. What if I give my mom another heart attack by upsetting her? I'd better soften this.

"Mom, I'm okay. I just had a hard day at work. I'll call you later, all right?" She reluctantly hung up.

The good thing about thinking that I had control of my life was believing that my every word, action, and thought kept the entire world in balance. The down side? One wrong move, and the whole world would fly into a million pieces. At a minimum, all my loved ones would die, my house burn down, and my underarm deodorant stop working. As I continued my slow crawl through Washington, I was left thinking about how I had misused my awesome powers of control and perhaps mortally wounded my mother. (Actually, she was fine. I apparently don't control the whole world.)

What a Wreck

As I inched into the K Street tunnel, I dried my tears and attempted to buck up. The line of red lights ahead of me looked as if it went on to infinity. Behind me I saw only autos and federal-style architecture. Downtown was nearly in total gridlock.

Bam! I couldn't believe it. The car behind me had suddenly rear-ended me. I was startled by the strength of the impact, considering the snail's pace at which we were traveling. How could anyone run into another car that hard in all this traffic?

Since I was a small child, I'd had a fear that if I was ever in a wreck, my car would burst into flames. Instantly I was in panic mode. This should have enabled me to get out of the car quickly—except that in my terror I tore the interior handle from my driver's side door. In disbelief I looked down at the useless piece of plastic in my hand. Rolling down my window, I grabbed the exterior handle and opened the door. My expression at the other driver must have included a wild-eyed stare as the man sheepishly approached.

He apologized profusely. "Sir, I am so sorry. I was looking at the ceiling of the tunnel and lost track of how far ahead you were."

The other driver's sincere apology disarmed me, and my anger turned to concern over the damage to my bumper. The man quickly wrote down his insurance information. I gave him my intimidating business card with the three-letter agency embossed on its face. The damage to my bumper looked minor, and I indicated that I might not bother turning it into the insurance company. He looked worried but got back in his car.

Since driving less than a mile from my workplace, I'd gone from stressed out to crying to freaked out. Now I grew strangely calm. I climbed gingerly back into my car, nursing my whiplashed neck. I didn't see how I could possibly make it to Tyson's Corner and my elders' meeting by seven thirty.

Traffic finally loosened up, and I sped past the Kennedy Center and over the Teddy Roosevelt Bridge. Once on the lush George Washington Parkway, I marveled at the beautiful old trees that flanked its sides. My mood was lighter now, and I thanked God for the glimpses of wildlife along the way. Somehow I arrived at the meeting only five minutes late.

Fatalism and Frustration

Fortunately, I hadn't missed a golden moment of the testy discussions about the future of our apparently dying assembly. Should we hire staff to focus on evangelism? Should we merge with a younger congregation and turn our property over to them? Should we just keep praying and see what happened?

Almost all these meetings left me frustrated. I'd joined the elders a year earlier in the hopes of making a difference and helping put the church on a better path. The other elders, however, seemed ready to give up and turn out the lights. It was hard being a younger elder. I was expected to defer to the elder elders, or at least the eldest elder.

Don't get me wrong, these guys were terrific people. I'd seen each of them make significant sacrifices personally and professionally for the good of the gospel. My beef was really about the fatalistic attitude. It was as if there was no hope in trying to fix the broken congregation. When I had agreed to be an elder, I'd had one main concern: I didn't want to join the leadership team only to have all the baby boomers retire and head for the hills and find myself presiding over a failed organization.

At this meeting the pastor was again pushing a merger with a small, younger congregation. While I recognized the beauty of a merger, I didn't have a good feeling about the fit of the two congregations. The other church's praise band played their music extremely loud, while our group preferred older choruses played energetically but well below one hundred decibels. Their group gave heavy weight to "words from the Lord," while our congregation put sound Bible teaching first. Their leadership seemed to have control issues, while our group included many free spirits. It felt to me as if the other group, led by its pastor, was aggressively attempting a hostile takeover—backed up by "words" from God that they had received.

Why wasn't God telling all of us the same thing? I'd never experienced an instance, up to this time, when God had told someone else that I was supposed to give them something without God telling me too. I had the Holy Spirit living inside me. This didn't make sense. But whether I was right or wrong and whether this idea was God's or man's concoction, it now looked as if the merger was going to happen.

As I climbed back into my car after the meeting, I felt as if my time on the elder board was being wasted. What was God saying to me? Why weren't we elders able to agree or at least disagree more amicably? Was it because we were just passionate over something that meant a lot to all of us? The worst of it was that our church did not have time to thoroughly think and pray all this through. Our congregation was bleeding members, and it looked like only a matter of time until the lights would go out.

The pressure of this matter added one too many things on the plate of my life. I wanted to be used of God, but all the anxiety and tension were getting in the way. Instead of a delicious banquet, my life was beginning to feel like a bad trip to the Golden Corral buffet: I was being forced to eat more and more—and none of it was satisfying.

2

THE ANXIETY BEGINS

ALL THIS TENSION had started three years earlier. I had been working for the Navy, doing contracting policy work in the Office of Naval Research, and I had become extremely bored with my job. While I loved the people I worked with—I had been there for more than twenty years—my work had become routine. I could do it in my sleep most of the time. It was so bad that I worried my brain would rot if I stayed another ten years until retirement.

So I started looking for a new job. I came across a few interesting possibilities, but nothing seemed as exciting to me as a certain fledgling three-letter government agency.

I applied, and to my surprise, I received a call rather quickly. I did not feel particularly suited for the first job they offered but was soon offered a position as a division director in a contracting shop. As a second-line supervisor in the field of contracting, my job would be to ensure that hundreds of millions of dollars were put on contracts each year and that other ongoing contracts were managed well from the government's perspective. I had four associate directors to help me and about fifteen other employees in my division.

Leaving the Navy was emotional for me. My identity had been immensely caught up with this branch of the armed services and its traditions. I had a drawer full of awards, medals, pins, and mugs. I had clothes—shorts with the Navy emblem, hats from a ship I'd visited, and shirts. I even had Christmas ornaments. But my pictures and memories would have to tide me over, because I needed to go. Moving on was like leaving home.

I had worked with many people in the Navy whom I admired. One of my first great bosses was a man named James Carbonara. He had taught me so much about respecting people, breaking down tasks into their smallest component, and measuring incremental success. Unfortunately, he passed away just before reaching retirement. He wasn't the only one who died while I was there. One co-worker drowned on a fishing trip, and another committed suicide over a perceived health problem. Leaving my Navy family severed ties to a large piece of my history.

I'd worked for the same man, directly or indirectly, for more than twenty years. He too was a great leader in many ways. He had kept things running smoothly while avoiding unneeded drama. Some found it hard to fully appreciate his calm style and wisdom until they experienced how crazy things could get under an excitable leader. I didn't know it, but I would be going from an ocean of calm to a madhouse.

The Navy gave me a big, fun farewell party. I embarrassed myself by crying (which was actually expected by those who knew me).

Afterward I felt as if I'd been to a party and funeral combined—but there was no turning back.

An Inauspicious Beginning

My first week at the new agency was a tough one. While I was excited to start something new, a bizarre health problem caused a major disruption to my new employment scenario.

As embarrassing as it is to admit, my rear end was burning like it was on fire. As my first week at the new job progressed, walking, standing, and finally lying down became unbelievably painful. I had to make it through orientation lectures, security briefings, and exchanging pleasantries—all while wondering if anyone had ever died of an inflamed rectum.

At first I suspected hemorrhoids, but I had never had one that hurt like this. Talk about roid rage, this was one of the most painful things I'd ever endured. And I *couldn't* talk about it.

Somehow I made it through the week, one day at a time, but by Friday night I couldn't sleep a wink. No matter how I positioned myself, pain shot through my body. Early the next morning I drove myself to Holy Cross Hospital in nearby Silver Spring, Maryland—a grave mistake.

When I arrived at the emergency room, the staff ushered me to an emergency room bed and pulled a curtain so I could disrobe. The attending physician was the first to get a look at my bum. He seemed horrified and began questioning me about my sexual habits. It was hard for me to understand him at first because of his thick foreign accent. I explained in detail that I was single, a Christian, and had not been engaged in any such activities. He left the room muttering, with me lying facedown in the prone position. My rear end was quite exposed, pointing to heaven. The doctor had asked me not to move.

Next a nurse came in and eyed my red, inflamed rear. This African American nun shouted to the doctor out at the nurse's station,

"There is no way I'm touching that with a ten-foot pole. Not with all that down there."

I didn't know what they were talking about, and I became extremely worried. Was my posterior in such bad shape that even these medical professionals were flabbergasted? Had my tush stumped the best that the archdiocese could assemble in our town?

The doctor entered again and put the screws to me about what had *really* caused this. Obviously I had been up to something perverse that had caused this crazy swelling. He was pretty sure it was venereal disease and that I was a scum-of-the-earth individual.

"Absolutely not," I said. "You have the wrong guy. There is a 'do not enter' sign back there."

"Well, something caused this," the ER doctor said as he departed in a huff.

And that's what I'm paying you for, I thought to myself. I lived in a day and age in which gays were getting married, and I had gotten the one hospital in America where they wouldn't fix my bum because they suspected I'd been using it for something besides ejecting Happy Meals.

The nurse and doctor conferred outside my room. I was getting increasingly upset that they thought this was a result of debauchery to which I had not been a party. Again I had been left lying there with my delicate hinder parts exposed. I heard the doctor and nurse discuss calling a surgeon, since the nurse didn't feel up to hacking at the inflamed area.

When the surgeon arrived, he greeted me and my rear end with a pleasant hello. *Finally someone who is not rear-end averse*, I thought.

The young doctor began to set up shop as if he was going to build a pinewood derby car. When he had his knives and saws and needles, he put a large pad under me and made his first entry. I nearly hit the ceiling as I shrieked in agony. He noted that he would need to drain the area, which was obviously filled with infection. He asked if I had been involved in that sexual activity that the others suspected. I assured him (now the third medical professional) that I had not been satisfying myself in this way.

To say that it hurt when he went to work would be to understate the obvious. I screamed like a schoolgirl at recess. He dug around back there for at least twenty minutes while I yelled, cried, and eventually sobbed into my pillow. Before going on break, the surgeon felt compelled to show me that he had drained enough pus out of my hinder to practically fill the twenty-four-by-thirty-six-inch pad. The pad was a kaleidoscope of color. I almost hurled.

After his unceremonious draining, the surgeon and the doctor determined that I could not take anymore. While the surgeon was not done draining and cleaning the affected area, my blood pressure was soaring, and he must have remembered from watching *Animal Planet* that a young hippo had died under similar circumstances. The staff decided to prep me for surgery and have me stay the night. I was less than eager to give them another eighteen hours to torture and insult me.

The ER doctor came to speak to me. At first he mumbled about standard of care and used several other buzz words; then he gave my diagnosis: my problem wasn't venereal disease, it was a thrombosed hemorrhoid. The ER doctor became sheepish since he had convinced himself, the nun nurse, and the surgeon that the cause of my woes was promiscuous sexual activity. My glucose levels were elevated, he explained, and this had caused the problem. It seemed as if there was something the doctor wasn't telling me, but I wasn't sure what.

Even with the good news that I had a reasonable explanation for my hinder parts being on fire, I still dreaded this hospital knocking me out and operating on a sensitive region of my body. I didn't trust them much at this moment. I also felt better. Draining of the aforementioned pus had relieved much of my pain. The swelling had apparently diminished—I say "apparently" because a man of my body type can't exactly see what's going on back there without a mirror or two. In light of these two factors, I wanted to go home. These people had been mean, rude and judgmental.

After a phone consultation with my sister, a nurse, I decided to throw caution to the wind and let them anesthetize me. The surgeon would go in, look around a little farther down the Hershey highway, and finish cleaning the site of the abscess.

All went smoothly, and I woke up in my room some hours later, in the middle of the night. Due to my excessive yelling in the ER, I had been labeled a screamer, and the staff had decided to dope me up on morphine, whether I needed it or not. In the witching hour, another scary-looking nun came into my room and drew close to my bed. Her face took on an evil glint as she inserted the morphine into my IV.

In the morning I was only too glad when the hospital discharged me to drive myself home. Apparently it was no problem for me to drive on morphine. Once I pulled out of my parking space, though, it was clear that something was not quite right. The car moved as I expected—and so did the trees and sky. I also had a heightened awareness of the beautiful colors around me. It was probably a good thing that I lived only a couple miles from Holy Cross Hospital.

Another Shock

The next morning I woke up in full withdrawal from my pain medications. I didn't have pain so much as a depression more intense than I had ever felt before. *Was I completely unloved and unwanted.* My urgent prayer for understanding begged God to know what was going on, and the Holy Spirit whispered to me that I was coming off the morphine. *Oh, that's why people like to stay on morphine once on it*, I thought. This eased my discomfort somewhat. The negative feelings remained, but at least I understood the reason for them.

Falling back to sleep, I worried about the future, specifically about how I could participate in the rapture of the saints, since I was afraid of high places. Would an acrophobic like me be able to meet Jesus in the air when He came back to Earth? My fears may seem silly, but they are real for me.

In my angst God found a way to make my terrible experience at hospital a little better. As I began to wake up from my sleep, I had an amazing dream that I took as a direct answer to my question.

I was riding in a school bus. Suddenly I knew that the bus was going to crash. I stood up to take the wheel from the bus driver, who had keeled over, but a voice said to me, "Don't worry about it."

"Don't worry about it? We're about to crash!" I said.

"It just doesn't matter," the voice said.

In an instant I threw my arms straight up and flew out the top of the bus. In a split second I was gone, and in my heart I knew that my fears didn't matter anymore. The crash didn't matter; my fears about the rapture and flying didn't matter; my withdrawal pains didn't matter. God would take care of me. I would find my faith tested on this point, however, in the days and weeks to come.

Being at Holy Cross had been extremely exhausting, and battling the abscess for a week afterward added to my exhaustion. While I was off work that week nursing my wound, my family physician called me.

"Mr. Winters, when you were in the hospital, the staff ran some tests. You have diabetes." He went on to explain that my abscess had been caused by elevated blood sugar. My blood glucose was over two hundred—double normal.

I was stunned and babbled incoherently into the phone. The doctor explained that many good medications for diabetes existed, and he would start me on one called Actos shortly. For the near term, at least, my condition could likely be controlled through medication, weight loss, and better eating habits. He would enroll me in the diabetes education program in the hospital where he practiced.

The news rattled me to the core. I'd long known that my excess pounds could lead to bad things, but this was more than I had bargained for—particularly at my age.

I had landed at my new agency with incredibly bad timing. My momentum for taking my new job by storm and starting well had been derailed. Suffering from the abscess, walking around in pain for a week, and being tormented by Holy Cross would have been a scarring enough experience in itself, and unfortunately it had happened just as I had left Navy and my work friends. To top it all off, I was now a diabetic and would have to stick myself daily. I would have to take medication and perhaps even lose a foot or a hand someday. Health fears piled on top of my concerns about performing well at my new job.

3

BUILDING PRESSURE

WHILE I ENJOYED WORKING FOR THE GOVERNMENT, I quickly discovered that my new agency job produced a much more stressful atmosphere than my Navy job had.

At work the Monday after the hospital ordeal, I walked to my office and began looking over the weekly workload report. It was August 2009, near the end of our fiscal year, when pressure always mounted on those of us in the contracting business. Customers wanted their projects funded, their supplies bought, or their support contracts renewed. Everything grew more urgent. One of my associate directors appeared in my doorway and quite obviously checked my mood before entering and sitting down. It was a simple thing, but this was a watershed moment for me. His action brought me severe guilt pangs. Hadn't I always been nice in the past? Hadn't I promised myself not to become one of those moody directors whose employees walk on eggshells? Did my open door have a force field around it saying "Turn back—ogre ahead"?

"Burt, come in and sit down," I said as amiably as I could. "I've always got time for my best employee. But don't tell the others I said that." It was my modest early morning attempt at humor with a message. The "sibling" rivalry between my employees was a little amusing to me because it was so juvenile. They competed with each other constantly, though there was no reason to. The rewards in government are pretty much the same for all directors—slim and none.

When I had arrived as division director three years earlier, the work environment had been toxic. Contracting employees fought internally. Customers were overly zealous in their expectations, and almost everyone blamed someone for something. My first job was to calm everyone down, weed out the particularly dysfunctional elements, and encourage better behavior. It was a big culture shift for some. As much as certain people liked drama at work, I didn't. My goal was to remove inappropriate emotion and reinforce intelligent, reasoned decisions.

Burt mainly wanted to chitchat and discuss minor procurements that were coming to a head. He briefed me as a courtesy and to ensure that I wouldn't later contradict him—though that wasn't really my style.

As Burt exited, Darren barged in. Darren was smart, sassy, and full of himself. Another of my associate directors, he always knew what everyone should do next and didn't mind telling them so. It wasn't bluster. He reminded me of Jane Craig in the movie *Broadcast News* because he was usually the smartest person in the room.

Today he was mad about a new policy missive. "What the &$%@@# are they thinking!" he bellowed rhetorically. "This is the stupidest thing I've ever heard. Doesn't this analyst know that you

never do this kind of thing this close to the end of the fiscal year?"
As Darren ranted, I tuned him out. I didn't want my blood pressure
escalating for no reason. I knew that policymakers (having been one
once) didn't always have the firmest understanding of operational
pressures; at times we had to take their policies with a grain of salt.
Certainly this gem was not worth an aneurysm.

As I tuned back in, Darren was expressing in vivid detail what he
thought the analyst was doing to him personally with this policy.
I blushed. It occurred to me that employees outside my closed office
door could no doubt hear his loud ranting, so I sought to calm him
down by probing deeper to discover his underlying frustration.
Eventually it became obvious that Darren was fearful—mainly
because he cared about doing a good job. He worried that these new
unrealistic expectations would be used against him at performance
appraisal time. While the news media painted us government types
as lazy slackers, the vast majority of federal employees I'd known
had gone about their jobs with great eagerness and professional-
ism and cared a lot about the results of what they accomplished.
(I always chuckled at political candidates who wanted to be pres-
ident of the United States but began their campaigns by railing
against their would-be future employees.)

I tried to reassure Darren that I knew he was giving it his all.
He began to cry in my office, as several others had done over the
preceding two years. The pressure in our department was getting to
him. Our work was difficult, the pressures many, and the comforts
few. Staffing was way too lean, and vacations were impossible to take
without returning afterward to an avalanche of unintended consequences. It was possible for us to work twelve to fourteen hours a
day if we wanted. (I *didn't* want—nine was enough for me—although
I was there ten or eleven hours too often.) The toll that our office
environment took on my employees gave me many opportunities
to use my psychology courses from The Ohio State University.
I always kept tissues close by.

My meeting with Darren had to end, as I was being called by the man upstairs. Not God, just one of the top leadership guys who sat a few floors above my office. Darren gathered his composure and wiped his tears. I felt inadequate as he stood to leave; I wished I could make those in leadership over me understand how much we needed additional staff. Darren called me "Pollyanna" and left quietly.

I put on my best Pollyanna smile, grabbed another employee to accompany me, and headed to the elevator.

Attacked by Anxiety

As I waited in the elevator lobby, my cell phone rang. The insurance company for the other driver in my fender bender wanted me to bring my car to their collision center. The accident had happened just yesterday—I had hoped to deal with this later. If the other guy hadn't panicked and told his insurance company, I may not have even filed a claim. He probably didn't trust me—afraid I was trying to pull something. When would I have time to take my car to the collision center?

The elevator hummed politely as my employee and I rode to the inspector general's suite of offices. I liked all three of the investigators who would be in the meeting, though we occasionally disagreed on this action or the meaning of that memo. But they had a job to do, and as a taxpayer, I was glad that someone was trying to make the government run better.

We all sat down at a ridiculously large table with comfortable office chairs. Immediately I knew that I was not well. My fear of heights had reared its ugly head as I had exited the elevator, and now it threatened to overcome me. Several minutes into the meeting, my head was swimming, and my stomach didn't feel right. My brain told me that the ship of my body was about to run aground. Warnings were going off about every system in my personal biosphere. Heartbeat was irregular. Breathing was shallow and difficult.

Stomach was spitting acid. Something terrible was going to happen. I needed to flee the room. Run away.

I felt as if a chemical was being released in my brain. Maybe I was about to pass out. Was this the big heart attack I'd been expecting?

But I had no pain in my chest, and my arm didn't hurt. Maybe nothing is wrong, I thought. But it felt as if my nervous system was about to shut down. What was that chemical seeping into my brain? *Am I going nuts, or is this just some kind of physical problem?* I wondered. A cord seemed to tighten around my cerebral cortex. This is how I'd felt when my mother had been talking to me in the car the previous evening—only more intense. I pushed back from the table and announced abruptly that I didn't feel well. "Could I have a glass of water or something?" My face drained of color, and I was unsteady in my chair.

All three of my interrogators looked concerned and even a little panicked by my sudden illness. The leader jumped up and went for a cup of water. My employee began to shake a bit.

I stood up, hoping that a change in posture might make everything right with the world again. Suddenly everything returned to normal. The attack, or whatever it was, subsided almost as suddenly as it had begun. I drank the water and sat back down. As everyone calmed down, I suggested we continue the interview. My hosts briefly protested, but I promised to see my doctor soon, and they relented.

"You're sure you're feeling better?" the lead investigator asked.

"Yes," I replied. "I won't die on you. It would look bad: 'Investigators Grill Director to Death in Plush Washington Office.'"

The g-men and the lone g-woman laughed nervously at my humor. *I like investigators who have a sense of humor*, I thought. We continued the meeting until they had exhausted their questions and themselves.

As soon as the interview was over, I returned to my office. Closing the door behind me, I got down on my knees behind my desk and began to pray. "Lord, what is going on in my body? I feel like

I'm losing my grip on reality. Is it the pressure? Is it something physical? Help me to find out. Whatever it is, help me to get better soon. I can't be crying when I call my mom. I can't be falling apart in business meetings. I have to get a grip. Please show me how."

Before I could say amen, the door swung open, and my boss barged in.

"What are you doing down there, Winters?" the colonel asked.

"Praying for strength," I said truthfully, though the colonel took it as a joke. "No one here but me."

"I guess we'd have a whole different set of problems if someone was down there with you," the colonel said, trying to interject humor.

"Yes, sir." As I got up from the floor, the colonel handed me an e-mail he'd printed out.

"I need a response within an hour. The Hill wants to know the status of this procurement. Pull the string on it, and get back to me as soon as you can."

"No problem," I said mechanically. Within a few minutes I'd dashed off a draft response and was on with the rest of my day.

The collision center answered the phone on the second ring and I made an appointment for them to evaluate the damage to my car. Add another stop on my way home this evening.

Adding Insult to Injury

One meeting led to another while tasks remained undone on my desk. At each meeting I felt more impatient than at the last. Small details dominated the conversations, and I saw no end of all the talking. Many great books about how to hold a productive meeting exist; unfortunately, most business people haven't read them. If only it were appropriate to lie on the floor and play with my toes over my head. It would have been just as productive.

Finally back at my desk, I began answering voicemail messages while reading the subject lines of e-mails of the one to two hundred e-mails that had rolled in that day.

As the morning turned to afternoon, hunger pangs reminded me that it was lunchtime. The extra weight I'd gained had to be ignored, as I didn't have time to locate truly healthy food in the neighborhood around my office. I decided to grab something in the small deli outside my office building and bring it back to my desk.

The Ethiopian shopkeepers were happy and pleasant as they rang up the other customers' orders. I ordered a Rueben and fries from the short-order cook, Laura.

"You look like you have the weight of the world on your shoulders," Jeff McMaster said to me with malice as I stood in line to pay. Jeff was one of our organization's particularly surly customers. He never said anything blatantly hostile to me but always had something discouraging to say. I decided to ignore his comment and asked him how he was doing.

"I'm great. Did you hear about our new Delta X program? We're really going to need your buyer's help to bring this in on time and within budget."

"Elizabeth is handling that one," I said. "She has it under control. Let me know if you see anything she's missing or anything not happening on time. I'm happy to meet with you."

I was relieved to get to the cashier and pay for my meal. The slender woman took my money with a beaming smile and returned my change. Her beautiful face and pleasant nature was like a drink of water in a barren land.

Little did I know what trouble lurked at the condiment bar. Suddenly, my hand began to tremble as I put the small condiment container up to the ketchup spout. Unbelievably, I was having a flashback to a previous battle so many years ago. Can one get post-traumatic stress syndrome from a condiment?

Year ago when I first started working for the Government, I'd ordered fries with my meal. After paying, I set my food down in front of the ketchup dispenser as I looked for the small plastic containers and lids. Before I could retrieve one and pump the delicious red concoction onto my waiting fries, a young woman came hurrying up beside me. She actually reached around me with her French fries and held them well below the ketchup spigot. Okay, *I can wait for you to use the ketchup before me*, I thought. *I'm sure you have some brain surgery to get back to.*

The woman used her free hand to enthusiastically pump the lever, but unfortunately the ketchup, almost magically, jumped over her fries and nailed me right in the crotch of my pants. We both stood staring, first at my pants and then at each other. Neither of us could think of anything to say. The woman apparently thought it would be inappropriate to wipe the ketchup off in light of its strategic location. Instead of getting me a napkin or even apologizing, Madame X pumped the ketchup dispenser again, took her fries, and evacuated the scene. I stared disbelievingly at my groin region. The red ketchup was seeping through my khaki-colored Dockers. Wow. *That looks bad*, I thought.

"Oh, I'm sorry," the cheery cafeteria worker said sweetly as she rushed to my rescue and handed me a few napkins. I dabbed myself dejectedly and walked shamefacedly away from the condiments. Carefully placing the bag containing my lunch at waist level in front of me, I limped dejectedly back to my office. Maybe this was the root of my ketchup battle scars.

Or maybe my phobia came from when I was a young teen, my parents and I were touring the fabled Underground Atlanta. A hobo drew close to me and pretended to stumble into me, leaving a swath of what appeared to be blood on my arm. I growled at him and showed my mom, but she and Dad were both unconcerned. Another time, in San Francisco, a man pinched my rear on the cable car to Fisherman's Wharf. My parents, apparently not well read at the time, didn't believe that a man would pinch another man's, or in this case a boy's, behind. It definitely happened to me and the man even smiled when I looked at him. Both of these insults were doubled for me because my parents failed to comfort me afterward.

I could deal with minor stressors when life was otherwise in relative equilibrium, but with multiple bad things happening over time, these kinds of small disasters were toppling me into a bad place psychologically. My busy, pressure-filled life was snowballing into something I couldn't handle.

4

A Broken What?

AFTER A TOUGH DAY I was particularly happy that I had dinner planned with a close friend that night. Nothing made me happier than one-on-one time with a good buddy, a great meal, and laughter. After a quick shower, I was almost dressed and ready to go. The mirror beckoned me for a look at my always hopeless hair situation. As I nailed down the few remaining tufts on top of my head, I noticed my long-ago broken nose that had never healed right. It wasn't Quasimodo disfigured, but it definitely tilted to one side.

My mind wandered back to that fateful Thanksgiving. It had been one of my goofier injuries. Life had been pretty dry that year—

a couple relationships hadn't worked out. I was feeling a bit lonely, so I decided to make lemonade out of the lemons life had given me and invited several friends to my small rental house for a traditional Thanksgiving dinner with corn casserole, green bean casserole, and any other kind of casserole that went with turkey.

That morning I bought all the groceries, including the maximum size turkey that would fit into the little oven in my galley kitchen. I prepared the dishes and planned to put them into the oven as soon as the bird popped its temperature-gauge thing. As I waited for the turkey, I washed food-prep dishes between trips to the living room to see plays of whatever pro-football game was going on that day. Pecan pie, baked the previous night, seemed to mock my growling stomach as I flashed in and out of the kitchen.

On one of my trips from the living room back to the dishes, I turned toward the kitchen just in time for my nose to crash into the firm plaster wall. My beak twisted to the right, and the pain was excruciating. My nose was crooked and broken.

Normal people would have turned off the oven, called their friends, and headed to the hospital. *I am not normal people,* I thought. *I'm tough—I'll gut this out. I didn't want to miss the food, the football, or the friends just to receive appropriate medical care.* I smushed my nose back in the right direction and had a great day with my friends.

It surprised me how many days it took for a broken nose to stop hurting, but eventually the pain subsided. (My nose is still just a little bit crooked.)

A Damper on the Evening

Having fully pondered the advent of my crooked nose in the bathroom mirror, I grabbed my keys and headed over to pick up my friend for dinner.

My friend and I sped to the trendy outdoor Rio Mall area. As we approached, it was obvious that many others had headed to Rio for their evening meal as well. In previous visits we'd spent many minutes circling the area for a parking spot, so I yielded to temptation and decided to park in the lot of an adjacent condo complex.

We both knew it was illegal and moderately immoral, but we were hungry and excused ourselves. All the legal spaces within a half mile appeared to have been taken, and other cars were circling, looking for someone to leave. This lot had at least a hundred empty spots. To our surprise, a guard stood at the entrance to this parking lot. Apparently they'd had a lot of trouble with illegal parking in the past (guilt twinge overridden—we weren't the only ones who had done this). I waved to said guard, who motioned me into the lot. I quickly pulled around to the other side of the main building and into a parking place. My friend and I laughed hysterically and walked quickly to the main thoroughfare. Normally I follow rules, all rules, all the time. This just seemed so fun and inappropriate for a responsible government official. We felt like naughty little kids.

There was a smidgen of mystery and intrigue in our illegal parking. Would we get away with it? Would we come back to an empty parking space? Would we be able to find the tow lot?

We moved like overweight, hobbled gazelles across a hilly grass berm that led to the restaurants. We headed stealthily toward the restaurants and picked up speed as we loped along. We continued laughing, feeling high from our minor sinful behavior. As we ran, we occasionally tried to say one thing or another between gasps for air. I mostly laughed at how immaturely we were behaving.

Our fun, unfortunately, ended abruptly. Due to a subtle (and then more pronounced) downhill portion of our course, I began to realize that I couldn't slow down. With my reverse thrusters not working, my nearly three hundred pounds went far faster than reason dictated. I tried to grab my friend's shoulder to slow down, but the more I reached toward him, the more he tried to get away from me, probably thinking I was going to do something goofy (a safe bet usually).

Laughing and running faster than my top speed, I couldn't get enough air to yell to my friend that I was out of control. Then, to my horror, the ground opened up before me. My foot went down twelve inches or so into a hole, stopping me instantly. I heard a loud, terrible crack from high up in my leg as I came down hard. Had I broken my femur?

I lay on the ground, and my friend hovered over me. "Are you all right?" he said concernedly. For a few moments, I was unable to speak from lack of oxygen and the hard impact I'd made with the ground. Joy was turned to depression in a moment.

"No, I'm not all right," I said bitterly a few minutes later. "Did you hear that cracking sound?"

We decided that I should try to stand before calling an ambulance. My friend helped me to my feet. To my surprise, I was able to stand and walk with difficulty. It hurt a bit, but my threshold of physical pain was pretty high. Not to mention I was slow to cancel when promised a meal at a restaurant. *Maybe I'm okay after all,* my inner dialogue began. *The last thing I need at this moment in my life is an injury. I can't miss work.* "Walk it off," my brain said robotically.

With steely determination I made it to the Red Mountain Grill. We would not miss out on dinner. My limp was noticeable, but we headed for a booth near the back of the eatery.

Courage evaporated the moment I sat down. The booth was not padded at this rustic-themed restaurant. I felt as if a bone were protruding out of my left rear cheek. Something was greatly out of alignment back yonder, as my Kentucky-born father would have said.

Thoughts of possibly needing surgery later that evening led me to order the salmon salad. *It isn't good to go to the emergency room too hungry or too bloated*, I thought reasonably. After eating half my salad, I limped out of the restaurant triumphantly. I was no party pooper. My friend had enjoyed a fabulous dinner while I had whimpered quietly into my tasty salmon salad.

Another Emergency Room

Back at home, however, self-pity came to call. Lying on my neatly made bed alone, the injury seemed untimely. Between the stress at church and at work and my burgeoning anxiety attacks, I felt under assault. "How could this happen to me?" I asked God. "Why me?"

With the pessimistic mood I was in, God didn't have much to say to me. Perhaps He figured I would see His larger plan later on.

My sister, the nurse, had told me years earlier that certain days of the week were not good for an emergency room visit. A lot of crazies showed up there on Friday and Saturday nights due to over-doses, knife fights, and other such goings-on. Being a Friday night, I waited through the night, trying to sleep with a bone jabbing at me.

At first light I got in my car and drove to the emergency room in Arlington, Virginia. No more Holy Cross for me! I was will-ing to drive the extra distance from Maryland to Virginia, where I had lived in the past and where the hospitals were much better (I thought.) As a former volunteer at the Arlington hospital, I knew a few people there, and my primary-care doctor practiced there as well. I felt as if I had home-court advantage over injury and illness at this hospital.

The nurses in the emergency room were skeptical that any bones were broken. "You couldn't walk if you'd broken a bone," they said encouragingly. "Let's just take few tests, and we'll get you on your way."

After a round of x-rays and blood tests, they changed their minds. "It turns out you did break something, sir," said Nurse Candy. "You broke your pubic rami."

I hadn't known that I'd had pubic rami. Now mine was broken. It turned out that the pubic rami was an important little bone that helped connect the hip to the femur. Apparently that big crack I'd heard was that bone chipping. Some tendons and a nerve or two were also dislodged. Since part of my pubic rami was still intact, the doctor gave me crutches, narcotics, and best wishes for a long and pain-filled recovery. I limped back to my car with instructions to see an orthopedic surgeon the following week.

My sister had been right. My visit to the ER had taken less than an hour.

I was dejected as I drove home. I wasn't in a cast and therefore couldn't escape the end of the fiscal year at work. Besides that, I was going to hurt a lot until this healed.

A follow-up visit to the surgeon indicated that there was no treatment for such an injury. I just needed to wait it out, and it would mend on its own. The surgeon consoled me with the uproarious coincidence that he had once experienced a similar injury while vacationing at some pricey resort in the Virgin Islands. *Ha ha*, I thought miserably.

The weird part about my injury was that it hindered my ability to lift my left leg. When I no longer needed the crutches, I sort of dragged my left leg along for several months. During this period my visage favored Igor from the *Young Frankenstein* movie. Small children ran in horror when they encountered me on the street. Scientists mispronounced "laboratory" as "luh-*boar*-a-tory." But over time, thankfully, I limped less and less.

My wise friend Hugh Boggs called these kinds of problems "pop-up annoyances." He believed that life was a series of pop-up annoyances. One could get all upset about them or just dig in and solve them as they came up. *Very healthy thinking*, I supposed. But some days I felt as if I had a few more annoyances than other people. Have I mentioned that these kinds of annoyances were overwhelming me?

I was already feeling stressed out with circumstances both at work and at church, which were fueling what looked a lot like panic attacks. Now a physical deficiency made all these things harder to negotiate. I was starting to get the idea that the world wasn't safe. Bad stuff was happening to me, and relief wasn't in sight.

5

THE PANIC

E VERYTHING WAS GOING FINE as I drove along the Capital Beltway one afternoon, when suddenly the alarm went off. "Get up, get away!" my panic told me knowingly. "You are dying!"

"I'm probably not dying," I told my panic, trying to stay calm. "I didn't die last time when you told me I was dying. What are the odds that I'm dying now?"

"Trust me," the panic said in a calm but intimidating voice. "You are definitely about to lose consciousness from this *heart attack*!" Panic shouted a little at the end because it saw that I might not take the appropriate evasive action to save my imperiled life from impending doom.

"No, look," I tried to say stoically. "This is just some chemical being released in my nervous system. It's imitating a heart attack. I've been to the hospital with this, and there is absolutely no truth to the idea I'm having a heart attack." As I said this, the chemical being released somewhere in the caverns of my large torso seemed to be seeping into my bloodstream to poison me.

My brain fuzzed up for just a moment, and then I was "gazelle intense," to borrow Dave Ramsey's term about running intensely from debt. Panic wanted me to pull over to the side of the road, but it would have been dangerous to do so where I was on the Beltway. I refused. Instead I slid down in my seat a bit to ease the pressure in my stomach. It worked, and a little relief was my reward. "God, help me," I prayed over and over for a minute or two.

The episode began to pass. I had felt as if I was in imminent danger, but no adverse consequences had resulted from the attack. I tried to take a deep breath. I couldn't for a few moments, but slowly my breathing became normal again.

Was I insane or just heading in that general direction? Was this happening because of too many twenty-ounce bottles of Diet Pepsi? Was the Aspartame killing me? A nutritionist had once told me that such drinks have excitotoxins, or something like that. (Of course, she had been trying to sell me her vitamin concoction, which may have affected her diagnosis.)

My family physician wasn't quite sure what to make of my attacks. I'd had occasional incidents like this in years past but never an ongoing problem until recently. I called my propensity to these episodes "the nuts thing," and whenever I complained about it at my annual physicals and occasional follow-up appointments, my doctor wrote me a prescription for a new pill. Most of these pills didn't help much, and I generally stopped taking them within a few weeks. If I ever had time, I planned to go the doctor specifically for this issue and make him take me seriously on it. After my freak-out in the investigators' conference room, *I* was serious about it. The doctor was going to listen to me, and we were going to find something that worked. There had to be an answer.

I hadn't just tried modern medicine. My friends had prayed for me. Ministers had used anointing oil, evangelists had rebuked the fear, elders had tried laying on of hands. Each of these had resulted in positive effects for a short time. Unfortunately, none of them had permanently fixed my anxiety problem or stopped the attacks from happening.

Pressures Mounting

My neighborhood has its challenges. I liked to refer to our neighborhood as just south of where the MS-13 gang met the Bloods and the Crips gangs. If only I were kidding. A few years ago, reported MS-13 members stabbed more than a half dozen people at the Target store a few blocks from my house. So in this place where houses sell for three hundred fifty thousand to seven hundred thousand dollars, we had a crime problem? How did gang members afford to live here? The crime in the area made me less likely to honk my horn in the streets around my house. This added a layer of pressure to simple things like taking a walk too close to sunset. To the South of my house is great prosperity and to the North poverty. Beggars line almost every intersection hoping to inspire generosity or at least, guilt. For me, it sometimes does both. I try to remember to pray, but often just shove a dollar out the window and try not to think about how this person fell on hard times. *What separates any of us from the beggar on the street corner*, I wondered.

Driving in DC traffic wasn't generally a pleasant experience either. I had a bent toward driving fast, as almost everyone on the Capital Beltway did (when we weren't forced to drive two to five miles an hour). Yet despite my competitive speed, about once a week someone raced around me on the one-lane entrance ramp. In their Ferrari or Porsche or other fine vehicle, they just couldn't stand to accelerate normally and flow into traffic; they had to hurl themselves onto the Beltway as if shot from a cannon. Why else would they have bought a Ferrari or Porsche? This meant entering the expressway could involve running into someone driving 30 mph or being run over by someone driving 70 mph on the entry ramp. Just commuting to work required courage some days.

While I truly loved Washington DC with its beautiful parks and historic landmarks and many good people, the stress of daily life in a crowded urban area fed the anxiety growing inside me.

Remembering

Arriving home from the store, I set my groceries on the kitchen counter and flopped on the loveseat. I was hopelessly exhausted. A football game took my focus from the pain in my pubic rami, and I imagined life without Washington, without work, and without pressure. I drifted off into an impromptu nap and dreamed comfortingly about my childhood in our big house on Madison Street in small-town Ohio.

My parents, though they had their faults, loved me well from an early age. In my dream Dad held me on his lap, and my head rested on his chest. I smelled the tobacco in his shirt pocket. It was a strong smell but comforting—it reminded me of his love for me. Our old green couch was cool to the touch on a similarly crisp autumn day.

The weather in my dream was like the weather I was then experiencing in DC: summer was turning to fall. Mom was coming out of the kitchen and drying her hands on a dish towel. *She always had fresh, pretty dish towels*, I thought. My older sister and brother were playing a board game on the floor, and *Gunsmoke* was playing on television. Mom was telling us that dinner was ready. We all came to the table in our large eat-in kitchen. The pork chops smelled so good, and a glorious pat of butter melted in the center of the large bowl of mashed potatoes.

Suddenly a loud crack woke me as a tree branch broke outside. A storm had come up while I napped, and a large, knotty branch from my tree had fallen harmlessly but loudly into the front yard. When it fell, the smaller sub-branches broke into many pieces. I was angry that my dream had ended abruptly, forcing me to remember the reality that my brother and father were no longer on this earth. I stared at the pieces of the dried out, dead branch. Was my life ending up in a similar state.

My brother, Buster, had been a fine man who loved his family very much. He was interesting and fun, quite a talker. So many people knew and loved him. Though he had been eight years older than I was, he had always been a must-see person on my visits back to Ohio. Buster was easy to admire because of his successes, his sense of humor, and his obviously caring nature.

For much of his life, Buster was outwardly extremely healthy. In high school he was an accomplished wrestler, losing only a few times in his three-year wrestling career. In adulthood he was a runner and eventually took up triathlons. In his final couple years, he badly injured his knee and gained thirty pounds or so. It was strange for me to see him physically unfit, and it clearly embarrassed him if anyone said anything about it.

Suddenly, however, Buster learned that his knee was healed. For months it couldn't support running, but on a lark, he decided to try to run again. No pain meant he could return to his routine. He was so excited that he could exercise and get fit again. To speed up his weight loss, he took ephedrine, an over-the-counter medication sometimes used to treat obesity, and perhaps other supplements. Buster threw himself back into running, and his excess weight melted off in just a month or so. He lost all the weight, 30 pounds, he'd gained over the course of a year. But the sudden change took a toll on him.

I was in bed one night when my phone rang.

"Hello—David?" It was my sister, Susie.

"Yes, it's me."

"I'm at the hospital," she said. It sounded as if she was crying.

"Is it about Mom?" I asked.

"No, it's about Buster."

"Buster?" That word made no sense in this conversation. If someone were in a hospital, it would be anyone except Buster. He hated doctors and hospitals. To my knowledge he never saw his doctor unless he was in major pain.

"He had a heart attack. He's gone," my sister said quietly. In the background I heard a cart roll down a hallway, an intercom blared an announcement. I said nothing. "Are you all right?" my sister asked into the silence.

"Yes," I said. "Let's talk in the morning."

"I love you," Susie said.

"I love you too."

I hung up the phone. This didn't make sense. It didn't compute. No way was Buster going to die before me. He didn't drink or smoke; he was an athlete. I was the chubby couch potato. Besides that, he was only forty-six. I started walking up and down the stairs in my townhouse. When life blindsides you, it is sometimes hard to know what to do. Emotionally I was thrown, and in some ways I never landed.

Besides the grief I experienced over the loss of my brother, the memory of his death became a lurking contributor to my panic. I was often afraid that I, who seemed far less healthy than my brother had, would have a sudden and unexpected heart attack. The fear I encountered during my anxiety attacks was very real.

6

A Vision of Peace

IT HAD BEEN EASY FOR ME to fall in love with Washington DC. My love affair with the city had begun shortly after college (and before I had experienced its metropolitan pressures!) when I had come for a job interview. Charles Colson's Prison Fellowship had been hiring for an entry level public relations specialist and they had flown me out from Ohio. Although my personal style hadn't impressed the staff at Prison Fellowship (primarily because they had worried that I didn't read enough news magazines to keep Chuck entertained), Washington had certainly impressed me. As my host drove me back to the airport through the beautiful forest along George Washington Parkway, I had prayed silently.

God, even if I don't get this specifc job, let me come back here some-day to live. God remembered my prayer.

Now, as a middle-aged man with a mending pubic rami who had been living and working in my dream city for twenty years, I began praying harder than I had in a long time. My strange anxiety attacks had continued for a couple months, usually triggered by heights or extreme stress, and I could see no immediate solution to the problem.

One morning at work I stood in the elevator lobby waiting for an employee who was coming with me to a meeting. As she walked toward me through the glass doors at the end of the hallway, I should have turned and pressed the button for the tenth floor. But my feet froze, and I couldn't easily turn toward the button. The meeting was starting in two minutes. My brain, or really my soul, just didn't want to go that high in our building, even though I went to that floor several times a week. My acrophobia suddenly took over. *What if I look out the window and freak out?* My stomach began to feel strange again, as if a chemical was being released. Was this the big one? Was I going to have a heart attack?

I wasn't sure how I had initially became afraid of heights. Maybe it was because my parents used to insist we go up in tall buildings on every vacation. Once we went up in a new skyscraper in Atlanta. The observation deck wasn't finished, and heavy plastic fluttered near where we were supposed to look out over the city. I was afraid and tried to stand close to my parents, but they kept moving away from me. I didn't know how to say "I'm scared out of my wits—help me."

My employee walked past me and pushed the button. She didn't seem to notice that I was having a momentary issue. When the elevator came, I got in, and we proceeded to the meeting. *Oh, no,* I thought as we walked through the interior hallways. Any open office door could allow me a glimpse of the tenth story of the building across the street. That's all it took to unsettle my mind and incite panic.

The person we were going to see, Tom, had an office with a lot of windows. He greeted us. Tom's deputy, my employee, and I sat at a small table by the window. I quickly took the seat nearest the window, ensuring that I would face away from the expansive view. Tom gave us his procurement requirements, and we talked about his issues and concerns.

I tried to concentrate, and my employee took notes. The strange feeling I'd had in the elevator lobby subsided as I concentrated on business and on the people in the room.

As Tom spoke to my employee directly, my mind wandered. I wasn't comfortable in Tom's office. A picture on the wall of woman's head with fifty or sixty strange piercings on and around her face disturbed me. Tom's daughter had taken the picture, and Tom was proud of her, but the piercings disgusted me. Not on religious grounds—I just hated piercings and got a creepy feeling from them. Since I sat facing away from the windows, I had to stare at this horrible picture. For some reason, it made me nauseous.

Thankfully, the meeting lasted only ten minutes. I retreated to my office and, once inside, shut the door.

Again I wondered if I was going nuts. Why in the world was I feeling this way, and how could I stop having these attacks? This time when I knelt next to my desk, I prayed audibly to the God of the universe. No answer came immediately.

The Beginnings of God's Answer

That weekend I looked forward to seeing two friends of mine: gospel singer Judy Dagraedt and her traveling companion, Mary Tack. Though our time together would be short as I ferried the two ladies to a retreat and other meetings, in those few days Judy was to have a profound impact on my life. God sent her as an answer to my prayer at just this time I needed her.

I had heard Judy sing previously on a mutual friend's CD, and the Spirit had led me to invite her to Virginia to minister at a retreat for the women of my church. She had accepted. Since I was already planning to be in Ohio for a few days just before the retreat, it was decided that I would meet Judy and Mary there and drive them the eight hours back to Virginia. I would then take them back to Ohio after the retreat. Though agreeing to two lengthy roundtrip drives was difficult for me in light of my pressures at work and other issues, it was God's perfect timing in my life.

Judy was a beautiful singer. As we drove from Ohio to Virginia, she put in some background tracks and sang one gospel song after another. The style was a bit old fashioned for me, but shining through it was the peace of God. Judy's voice spoke to me and gave me a sense of assurance that God was answering the prayers I'd been praying. I could hear the Holy Spirit in her voice and sense Him all around me. The presence of God's Spirit comforted me through this time with Judy and Mary, who was also a strong Christian.

Somehow the peaceful hours I spent with these godly women birthed the seed of an idea in me that I knew was God's answer to my prayers for relief. For the first time the idea that I needed some time alone with God to address the many emotional and physical issues that plagued me came to my mind. Perhaps I needed a retreat of some kind, a season away from my regular life during which I could face my fears and get to the bottom of them. The thought stirred in me a sense of hope.

As we started back to Ohio at the end of the weekend, we came again to the mountains of West Virginia. Worn out from the travel as well as the obligations I'd had over the weekend while the ladies were at their retreat, the euphoria I'd experienced during the previous eight-hour trip was not repeated. Still, God would use this drive to help me understand what I needed to do.

As we left a rest area about ninety minutes into our eight-hour journey, Mary questioned me about my first girlfriend, whom I'd mentioned in passing. Almost simultaneously we drove into a huge bank of fog. I tried to brush off Mary's questions about this girl (who was now deceased). Thoughts of her made me feel anxious, and the fog added to the intensity of the situation.

Perhaps not recognizing my angst, Mary persisted long enough to send me into a full-on anxiety attack. The now-familiar feeling of a chemical being released inside me led me to a sense of impending doom. Before long I pulled into a lonely park just off the highway and still in the mountainous region. The Forest Service outpost was deserted, and all of us were uncertain about our next move. No gas stations or businesses were to be seen. I felt closer to whatever event (whether a heart attack or meltdown) seemed likely to end my short but semi-illustrious life. The whisper of an unseen enemy told me I would not make it out of the mountains alive.

Trying not to scare my traveling companions any more than I had to, I excused myself by saying that I was feeling sick. Up and down the parking lot I walked for a few minutes until the feeling subsided a bit. The women talked in an animated way in the car. No telling what they were saying. I didn't want to know. Eventually I returned to the Impala and asked Mary if she could drive for a while. She agreed but seemed dissatisfied with my explanation of what was wrong with me. I too was unhappy with it.

It struck me as we drove along that even in the presence of these two Christian ladies, my encroaching malady had come to the fore. They prayed for me, and I felt a little better, but it was becoming obvious to me that I needed a deep healing. I thought again about the idea of taking time away from life to fix what ailed me. A weekend or two wasn't going to do the trick.

My Malady—and God's Solution

After leaving Judy and Mary in Ohio, I started back to my home in Maryland. Though I had said goodbye to the ladies, Judy continued speaking to me through her CDs as I popped one into my car's player and listen to her recorded testimony of a troubled childhood. Judy had painted a picture of utter chaos turned to perfect peace. Though I had accepted Christ long before, I began to see clearly that I needed to regain the peace I had felt when I had first believed in Jesus.

Though Judy's and my situations were different, Judy had diagnosed my malady: I had lost my peace and sense of well-being. Somewhere through the years, perhaps along a roadway or during a hectic Washington life, I had misplaced my personal peace. I didn't feel safe. Danger lurked, and I didn't know how to identify it. A basic center of well-being was missing from my life. While I'd had glimpses of peace, it had been missing from my life as a predominant quality for a very long time. So long, in fact, that I didn't even know where to look for it.

As soon as I returned home, my search began. I found that the word "peace" was used four hundred times in the King James Version of the Bible. In some respects I felt like a terminally ill man who was discovering the cure for his disease.

My initial study of some of these four hundred uses of the word "peace" revealed God's heart for me. The perfect peace of God was intended to be at the center of my being—but it was not. Jesus was in my heart; I was washed in His blood;

I was a Christian and sure of it. But still I didn't have peace in the midst of my storms, and I knew that no amount of man's medicine or psychotherapy could give it to me.

I needed personal time alone with God, and I needed it soon. It was the pathway, I felt certain, to deliverance from my attacks, to feeling well, to living rather than dying. But was it more important than my secure, six-years-from-retirement government job?

Judy had painted a picture for me of what was missing in my life: not salvation, not a relationship with Jesus, but the peace that passes all human understanding. When a sick man hears about a medicine that might cure him, he will fight very hard to get that medicine. That medicine is hope. It is life. It must be obtained. That's how I felt as I studied the peace of God. What was ailing me wasn't trivial; it wasn't the spiritual equivalent of a cold. Whatever was eating my lunch was more like a cancer than poison ivy. I became convinced that I needed time to commune with God—a lot of time—to receive His healing over a period of days and weeks.

7

CONTEMPLATING A PATH TO HEALING

NOW THAT I KNEW I NEEDED TIME APART to find a cure for my anxiety and to re-tool my life, I had to figure out how to obtain it. Should I take a leave of absence or quit my job outright? Should I step back from service positions or church responsibilities that engulfed so much of my time?

As I pondered and prayed, God whispered the word "sabbatical" to me, meaning a place of rest, a time away from the everyday demands and pressures of life. The sabbatical itself wouldn't be my cure—time with God would be. To get this time, I had to find a way to detach and unplug from the stressors in my life. I didn't want to get away from those I loved, but I did need to find time to be alone

The idea of having time away from the craziness of life was taking hold of me, but the seriousness of quitting my job gave me pause. If I was really going to leave my secure and well-paying government job in a stormy economy, I needed to know three things for sure:

- First and foremost, was this God's will for me right now?
- How would I pay my bills while I was off work?
- Did it make sense to quit my job in the middle of my career, and could I return to the workforce after the sabbatical?

Discerning God's Will

My first step was to imagine what a sabbatical would look like and pray about it. This was the path, I knew, to overcoming the seeming impossibility of such a big change. I needed to hear directly from God on this one.

I turned to the old standby methods of hearing from the Lord: prayer, reading the Bible, listening to preachers who taught from the Bible, hearing testimonies of Christians who had walked through difficult circumstances with God, praising God, and receiving counsel from Christian friends. I knew I might not immediately get the perfect answer for my situation, but frequent use of all these tools helped me talk to God and, much more importantly, helped me to hear from Him.

My personal devotions led me to passages about the active resting that God envisions for a sabbatical. I scheduled time with several Christian friends and mentors who knew me and who had taken time away themselves, and I asked their thoughts and advice. I also read the few articles about sabbaticals I could find that had to do with spiritual renewal.

As I talked to God daily about my desire for a sabbatical, all lights seemed to be green in the spiritual realm. Everything I read and everyone I spoke with supported the idea of a sabbatical for me now. There was no bright lights or angels singing, but in my heart and soul everything seemed to add up naturally.

Paying My Bills

Having a general peace from God about the idea of taking a sabbatical, I turned to a practical matter: how would I pay my bills if I wasn't generating income? My career wasn't at a key turning point—retirement for me was six years away. I knew I couldn't make it until then. I didn't want to ruin my finances to take a sabbatical, but I also didn't want to ruin my health by *not* taking a sabbatical. Still, eating and having a roof over my head were significant matters to consider.

The sensible side of my brain kicked in. Could I really swing this financially?

I had a lot of money sitting in my retirement fund. It occurred to me that I could live off that for quite a while. "But there are penalties for early withdrawal," my responsible self argued resolutely.

But the most dominant thought in my mind remained that I needed to stop the world and get off for a little while. It was becoming increasingly difficult for me to put one foot in front of another. I remembered Judy's vision of peace. If Judy Dagraedt could find peace in the storms of her life, maybe I could too. It might require giving up everything I had, but I was willing to go for it.

As I looked carefully at my savings, it looked adequate to finance a sabbatical for a year. I would need to consider other practical issues, such as health and life insurance and some personal debt, but I would address these matters. Short answer: I could afford it.

Career Considerations

But what about my career? Did it make sense for me to quit my government job six years before becoming eligible for retirement? And would I be able return to work after the sabbatical?

From my earliest years, I had been encouraged to compete with those around me. Like most other kids, I got all kinds of affirmation if I hit the ball farther, ran faster to the finish line, jumped higher over the illusionary hurdles than the next child did. I needed to keep my grades up so my future would be wide open. I had to gain admission to the right college or train under a great master who would give me credentials for greatness.

Success at certain levels eventually came my way—my job momentum carried me to a relatively high place in the career civil service. Now as a division director in a three-letter government agency, I was well paid for my efforts. But the momentum that had carried me to this point was now threatening to wash me out to sea. Something was very wrong with my life, and I needed to fix it. Suddenly I no longer cared about reaching the top rung of the ladder.

But could I give up my position, my colleagues, my routine? Work was my identity. It was a source of respect for me. I knew that announcing a sabbatical wouldn't make sense to some of my friends. Like a budding tennis star who has grown tired of the relentless grind, I would greatly appreciate a sabbatical, but some of my closest friends would doubt my choice. Was I ready to make such a decision and walk away from work?

As to returning to work after the sabbatical, I'd heard throughout my career that federal contracting people could always find a job if they were willing to take a little less pay than they may have received in the past. I resigned myself to the reality that this might happen to me. I already had a respectable high-three federal retirement plan, which would benefit me no matter which choice I made. If I came back to work at a lower salary—but amazingly healed and recharged—it would be worth any financial loss I might incur.

I started to know for certain that I was going to do the unthinkable: just a few years before eligibility for retirement, I would quit. It was not only possible but probable that I would take a sabbatical.

Timing

One of the tricky parts to taking a sabbatical, I discovered, was figuring out the right time to stop my life. In some ways it seemed as if there *was* no right time. Leaving my job immediately, just as the agency was approaching the end of its fiscal year, would be irresponsible of me, as this would make life difficult for my fellow employees. On the other hand, with a little planning, I thought I could figure out a conscientious exit strategy.

As I researched the possibilities, I saw similarities between ways a person's regular life could come to a stop and ways an airplane could land.

First, a life could crash. A sabbatical might begin unwillingly with a sudden job loss or an abrupt life change. As when a plane crash-lands on a desert island, this kind of start to a sabbatical would require a great deal of adjustment. After some time of realizing and analyzing what had happened, however, a person might just find that he's ended up in an island paradise and that God is able to provide everything he needs to relax into a sabbatical.

On the other end of the spectrum, a person could think ahead and invest extensive planning and savings into a sabbatical, as when a plane lands smoothly, safely, and on time as expected. Some jobs come with an opportunity for employees to take a sabbatical. In other cases life provides a windfall that may finance at least a limited-duration time away. If I'd had time to plan and if my finances could have been better arranged, this would have been optimum. Perhaps if I'd had this level of planning, I would have found a welcoming party with leis and cool drinks. That would have been a great way to begin a sabbatical.

Third, as was the case with me, a person could be forced quickly into a sabbatical due to some kind of pressure and have only a little time for planning. This is probably the most typical scenario. A plane is running out of fuel. A storm rocks the plane back and forth. Using radar, the pilot detects an island ahead; the plane's engine sputters as the fuel gets dangerously low. The plane dives out of the clouds as the pilot searches for visual contact with the island airport. Finally he sees it and lines up the approach. The wheels touch down hard, and the plane bounces on the runway.

The pilot slams on the brakes, and the plane skids to a halt, a bit askew. With relief the passengers exhale and applaud.

I didn't have time to work out all the details. I just knew that I was getting more nuts every day and that I needed time with God more than anything else. Still, stepping into a sabbatical this way took faith, because it was at least somewhat voluntary (unlike a crash landing would have been). Waves of rain and gusts of winds seemed to push my plane downward. I was much in doubt as to a safe landing until the last moment.

As I thought and prayed about the best timing for a sabbatical, a voice inside me seemed to tell me to do it sooner rather than later. The fiscal year would end in October, about two months from now, and that would provide an obvious break in the action at work. This would give me a little time to plan while giving me hope of relief in the immediate future.

Excited about the Possibilities

As the idea of taking a sabbatical became more and more certain for me, I thought about what a super-recharged me could accomplish. What if I wasn't obsessing about my fear of heights or having anxiety attacks? I wanted to think that my phobias weren't that noticeable, but surely my co-workers would notice a new and improved me if I came back to work rested and rejuvenated. Then again, what if I didn't come back to work at all? What if the right road for me led somewhere besides government? The thought almost made me giddy with joy. Could a sabbatical lead me to a whole new way of life? Could I reinvent myself and have a more creative, interesting world on the other side of the sabbatical?

I imagined my life after a months-long rest period of reading, outdoor adventures, and new spiritual insight. Things could be very different.

I also imagined the first day of a sabbatical. What would it look like? How would I feel the first work day after quitting my job? What new patterns would I install in my days to ensure a successful time away? I began to get excited. Whenever I thought about taking time away from life, I smiled. The subversive nature of it all. It was so counter-culture to stop striving for worldly success and calmly explore my dreams of what life could offer.

Perhaps it was a sign from God that none of my imagining led me to a place of fear. Instead I felt great peace. I had heard it said in Christian circles that one should follow his peace. What made me feel peaceful was to ride away from the stress and into the sunset, at least for now. As many risks as I saw in the idea of a sabbatical, it seemed to me a much bigger risk to remain in my current crazy life as my attacks grew more acute.

Regardless of all my considerations, I felt deeply drawn to take a sabbatical for one reason: I heard the Savior call to me, "Come away." He repeated to me the words from Song of Solomon 2:10: "My beloved spake, and said unto me, rise up, my love, my fair one, and come away."

Sabbatical—an Active Rest

While my body was still at work, my mind and heart were moving toward sabbatical. In my spare time I started studying the meaning of the word "sabbatical." What exactly did it mean? "Sabbatical" came from the Hebrew word *sabat*, which meant "rest." My sabbatical would be a time when regular work and the pressures of life were set aside for a time to find out about God, myself, my past, and my future.

I read Genesis 2:3: "On the seventh day, God ended his work which he had made; and he rested on the seventh day from all his work which he had made." This verse implied that rest was a good thing. It also implied that there was a correct proportion of working to resting. I shouldn't assume that only rest was good; this verse taught that both work *and* rest were good. I had been in the workforce long enough to learn that many in our postmodern world felt that retirement meant an end to work. But for a lot of people, retirement ended up being the short route to misery. I didn't want to be without purpose. I had no desire to give up work and quit accomplishing things. I wanted to work until I went to heaven. I didn't necessarily want to fight traffic or feel pressured to make deadlines, but I definitely wanted to keep on contributing to the common good and helping people. My sabbatical would be a time not to avoid work but to seek God about what kind of work He had for me down the road.

Exodus 34:21 provided a law for the Jewish people: "Six days thou shall work, but on the seventh day thou shalt rest: in earing time and in harvest thou shalt rest." Even as I continued working for several weeks more during this excruciatingly busy time of the year for my agency, I didn't want to fail to get at least some rest each week. This Scripture indicated that weekly rest was needed during the harvest time as well as during the winter months.

The Bible also talked about a sabbatical year. This was to be a year of rest for the land (and by extrapolation, for the people) every seventh year. Every so often people needed a longer break than just once a week. Even God's creation (the land) needed a break. Farmers know that it isn't healthy for land to be used year in and year out without rotating crops or fertilizing, and even though modern farming has made it possible to avoid letting land go fallow for an entire year, the principle of the land needing a break from the same routine remains the same today as it did in Old Testament days.

Scholars adopted the idea of a sabbatical in 1599 as a year away from teaching for rest, travel, research, and other endeavors.

The Webster's online dictionary definition of "sabbatical" that best fit my plans was "a break or change from a normal routine (as of employment)." As I concluded my study, I saw that "sabbatical" simply meant taking a rest from labors of obligation and actively pursuing meaningful time apart from everyday life. There were many ways that my life felt out of control, big questions went

unanswered because there was never time to even think. My sabbatical wouldn't be a season of unproductive time, even if it largely
turned out to be rest. In fact, it could become the gateway to a
whole new stage of life.

8

LET'S DO THIS!

E VEN AS MY THOUGHTS ABOUT LEAVING MY JOB began to take on a note of certainty, I yearned for further spiritual confirmation. All through the Bible, God had communicated with those who were looking for Him. This had been true for my circle of Christian friends as well. A very few times in my own life, God's voice had even seemed almost audible in my head.

The first time I heard this voice I was twelve or thirteen years old. I had gone to a Christian film and concert in a school auditorium. The movie was about a lounge singer who had gotten involved with pills and booze. He'd had a dramatic conversion to Christ and was now singing for Jesus. After the movie the singer came out and gave a brief concert. Finally he gave an altar call and asked who would like to accept Christ. I found myself crying. The speaker said that we should come down front if we wanted to receive Christ.

Even though I'd been raised in a Methodist Church that abandoned altar calls decades earlier, I strongly desired to go down front. A voice in my head urged me to go. I asked the voice, "Are You God?"

"Yes, I'm God," the voice said. "Now go down front, and they will tell you what to do."

I was overwhelmed. Just to know that there really was a God was mind-boggling. Holy cow! Who knew? There was a God, and He had taken the time to come from heaven to a cheesy concert in Ohio and save insignificant me. What could I do? I followed the voice's instructions and went down front to accept Christ. The trained staff led several of us into a back room and prayed with us. They gave us some literature, which I noticed immediately was from the Billy Graham Evangelistic Association. It dawned on me that I had just done what I'd seen so many thousands on television do. This must be the mysterious literature the announcer was always talking about at the end of each broadcast. I had always wondered what it said, and now I would know. Before this time, I had head knowledge about God. After this point, I knew there was a personal God who cared about me.

While hearing this almost audible voice in my head had been great, it didn't happen to me every day. More often an inaudible still, small voice pointed me in the right direction, convicting me of wrongs or comforting me in times of trouble. Now I faced a watershed moment in my life. I needed absolute confirmation that my decision to take a sabbatical was the correct one.

Hearing from God

I decided to go to the Vienna Christian Healing Rooms a ministry that specialized in helping people focus on God. They prayed with people to be healed, to hear from God, or to receive salvation. Whatever a person needed, they simply brought him or her through prayer to God's throne. Their slogan was "It's all about Him."

On a still, hot Saturday afternoon, I made my way to their meeting place. Though hot outside, the church sanctuary was cool. Those waiting for prayer were encouraged to sit in the large, mostly empty auditorium where worship music played in the background. As I waited, I prayed quietly and gazed at the large cross in the front of the room.

The prayer teams were made up of ordinary people who had received training and experience in listening for God's voice while praying for others. They began their sessions with an individual by praising God for several minutes. Then the teams prayed together with the individuals, seldom knowing who would show up or what needs would be presented on a given day. As a team finished praying with one person, a new individual was ushered in for a prayer session. They did not charge, of course.

My turn came up. Two women and a man prayed for me. I explained a little about my situation—that I needed guidance for a major life decision. I kept the details vague, however, and let God say whatever He wanted to tell me through these saints of His.

The first person prayed for God to heal my ears so that I would clearly hear Him in making my decision.

The next intercessor prayed for faith to arise in me. She instructed me to spend much time in Scripture to hear from the Word of God. She quoted a scripture that said faith comes by hearing—specifically by hearing the Word of God.

The third prayer warrior, as I had requested, prayed for my ankle, which I had sprained a day or so earlier. Though it wasn't the reason for my trip to the healing rooms, it did instantly feel healed. The guy also talked about taking a leap of faith—trusting in God. Normally his words may have seemed routine to me, but I was indeed in a situation that required a leap of faith. The man then quoted the old adage, "Jump, and the net will appear." In other words, I wasn't to wait for everything to be perfect. I needed to trust God. He was reliable and the whole sabbatical would require faith.

On my way home I marveled that my ankle had been healed miraculously. As I walked into my house, it felt completely well, and the next day the pain stayed gone. I'd taken a leap of faith to go to the healing rooms, and God had not only given me the confirmation I had sought but had healed my ankle as well. I was going to take this sabbatical and ride it for all it was worth.

Social Implications and Needs

My decision was made! This was really going to happen. If I was going to quit my job and take an extended period of time off work, I needed to start thinking about the practical implications.

As a people person, work for me was more than an opportunity to accomplish something great for our country. It was also a source of companionship and fellowship. The people at the agency where I worked were interesting, intelligent, and fun. Locking myself up in a room alone for months would not be healing for me. Whether I got involved in a volunteer project or simply handled mundane tasks for my church, my sabbatical would need to include people.

Part of my need for socialization could be filled by informal times with friends and a few regular commitments. One of those commitments, I decided, would be leading a weight-loss group called "Losing to Live" for the duration of my sabbatical. I'd been part of this competitive weight-loss program founded by local pastor Steve Reynolds. Now I would step up my game and take a leadership role. This would kill two birds with one stone: it would provide a regular small-group commitment with a smattering of people I already knew, and it would motivate me in my own weight-loss struggle.

My energetic resting could also include an aerobics class at the gym; this would be another way to stay connected with people. Right now I was almost always too tired to go to the gym. Once my sabbatical started, I would rest up and then go to the gym for a regular class at least once a week; I would also go most days by myself to work out individually.

I also had relatives whom I didn't see often enough. The sabbatical would give me a chance to plan some time in their towns or on vacation with them elsewhere.

As a single person, my home was not buzzing with other people unless I invited them over. In the past I had entertained a lot; cooking relaxed me, and having dinner guests brought me joy. The sabbatical would allow me time to do this again. I thought that I could invite a different friend over for dinner at least once a week (when I was in town) for the duration of the sabbatical. It would be fun to finally meet my new neighbors and make new friends and also to catch up with buddies from the past.

Church had been a big part of my life almost continually since I had moved to the DC area. I had no plans to discontinue that during my sabbatical. As I moved mentally toward a sabbatical, however, I felt that I needed to shed my elder responsibility at church. I'd seen how the sausage was made, and I wanted to become a "vegetarian." Giving up this post was a big spiritual decision for many reasons, but when it came down to it, I felt I could not handle the stress during my sabbatical. While I wanted to stay connected with my church, I didn't want to be on a treadmill of activities. The sabbatical was about getting off the carousel for a while.

Having completed an MBA several years prior to this, I decided against taking formal college classes during my sabbatical. It would be important for me to remember the primary purpose of my time away: rest. More commitments with deadlines were not right for me.

My support network included everyone from the staff at my regular barber shop to the members of my church to the people behind the counter at Starbucks. These people would help keep me connected socially, some on a daily basis. The value of a kind word resonates boldly in the fight against loneliness.

As I thought through my emotional and social needs, I recognized a big difference between planned solitude and accidental loneliness. The latter could be staved off by planning the right amount of interaction and activity during my sabbatical. While I shouldn't plan so much activity that I had no time left to be alone with God, I needed to build a support system.

Crunching Numbers

Another implication of quitting my job would be a need to make major adjustments in my monthly budget. Quitting work and going on a sabbatical might be fairly affordable for a person who didn't have a family and was debt-free, if that person found ways to greatly reduce expenses. Unfortunately, this was not my case. While I did not have a wife or kids to provide for, I did have considerable debt, including a house that was underwater and almost impossible to sell. I had bought the house with the intention of remodeling it and making a profit selling it, but the housing market in my neighborhood had collapsed, rendering my plans impossible. Actually, my favorite Scripture about finances was "Jesus wept." My financial path would not be entirely worry free with or without the sabbatical. Perhaps my willingness to turn this part over to God speaks to the urgency of my need for a sabbatical.

The articles I read about sabbaticals had some ideas on financial management for a person considering an extended time away from work:

- Live off savings.
- Sell something big (a house, boat, car, artwork).
- Agree with a spouse, parent, child, or close friend to live on their income.
- Borrow money (while you still have a job) to cover the sabbatical costs, and repay the loan when you return to work.
- If your home is paid for, sell it or rent it for the period of your sabbatical and live somewhere cheaper.

The most obvious cache of money for me was my government IRA-like account, called a Thrift Savings Plan. If I withdrew funds from this account, I could live pretty much as I had been living— without the encumbrance of a job. I also considered withdrawing enough from the retirement fund to pay off other debts, excluding my mortgage, although I wasn't yet ready to decide whether that would be the best use of my funds.

I had made a lot of my decisions prior to my sabbatical based on finances. But now I *couldn't afford not to* escape the rat race. My health was suffering, and I needed a way to refresh, recharge, and reenergize. Raiding my retirement fund is what I needed to do to survive.

I would face substantial tax consequences, however, for the early withdrawal of funds. While not everyone would feel comfortable returning to work haunted by a large tax bill, I made the choice to do it with eyes wide open.

While I clearly needed counsel in making some of these financial decisions, I knew I should discuss my plans only with a few trusted friends and family members. I had to be careful whom I confided in, particularly when it came to people who had connections to my work. I did confide in one person at work, a trusted former military man who was great at thinking things out and keeping a secret. He asked me good questions and helped me think through the ramifications of my actions. His advice was crucial in giving me the assurance that I'd covered all the important bases before announcing my departure.

Insurance

One of my concerns about leaving work had to do with health and life insurance coverage. Maintaining these key pillars of my personal finances would be vitally important. Confident now that I was all in for the sabbatical, I met with the personnel office at work to talk turkey and insurance.

The smiling human resources person laid out my options very clearly. The law required that I be able to continue my health insurance after leaving my job provided that I paid the premiums. The window for ongoing coverage would extend well beyond the six to twelve months I saw as the likely duration of my sabbatical.

All this was covered under a law called COBRA, which extended protections to employees who had lost their jobs and wanted to continue their health insurance. The bad news was that the cost of coverage was often quite a bit higher than what the employee had paid while still on the job. This was true for me. The Blue Cross premiums I had paid while a worker were approximately 170 dollars per month. On sabbatical my payments would jump to 550 dollars per month. This increase would be a significant budget hit—particularly if I extended the sabbatical beyond a handful of months.

While I would have to pay significantly more for health insurance, my transition to COBRA went relatively smoothly. Life insurance, on the other hand, was a fiasco. My human resources director literally bragged about my ability to continue my life insurance coverage after I quit, telling me that several private firms were just chomping at the bit to give me continued coverage at similar prices to what I'd been paying. She called this option a conversion. "Perversion" might have been a more accurate word.

In practice, the program for continuing life insurance barely existed. My first step was to procure a letter from the government stating that I was entitled to continue my coverage. Though I requested this, the letter was extremely slow in coming. The clock was running toward the time I would give notice, yet no one was in a big hurry to get me the letter explaining my options.

When it finally came, I was referred to an office in New York City. That company didn't answer their phone for more than a week, so I left a voicemail, which went unanswered. Eventually I got a hold of someone, and she didn't sound as if she knew much about the program.

As I listened to her unconcerned tone, I pictured the back of a dry-cleaning operation. "Hey, Butch," she spoke to someone in her office, "you know sumthin' 'bout temporary continuation of coverage life assurance?"

"No, Gert, I don't know nothin'."

"I'm sorry, sir, we got no info for ya," Gert said nonchalantly.

"Please," I appealed. "I got this letter from my government agency, and it says that the first step is to ask you for contacts at the life insurance agencies."

Although Gert feigned ignorance, she finally sent me a letter. It listed three companies that participated in this program and were supposedly standing by to convert my life insurance coverage.

As it turned out, these companies weren't that eager. The first one didn't "do that anymore." The second, New York Life, had an office near me, so I went for an in-person meeting on one of my few remaining days off. To get term life, they wanted me to take a physical. If I wouldn't answer a questionnaire and take a physical, they would grade me as if I were a smoker and charge me their highest price for term life. That price was about double what I had been paying, and it offered about a third of the coverage.

My last resort was a North Carolina life insurance firm that was very much up to the challenge. While they did only offer me whole life, it was much less expensive than what New York Life charged and offered a better rate of return for my investment. This firm had been around a long time and appeared to have a strong financial footing. I felt confident choosing them and began the signup process to avoid a break in coverage.

Confirmation from the Lord and many practical details were beginning to converge and move me toward a sabbatical. I was both nervous and excited, but mostly excited.

9

COUNTING DOWN THE DAYS

IN EARLY SEPTEMBER I gave notice to my bosses. My shocking announcement generated the expected combination of stunned silence, kind words, and instructions to stay in touch.

I told my direct supervisor first. He was extremely surprised and said all the right things to make me feel wanted and to encourage me to thoroughly consider my decision. I waited another week before giving my formal notice. When I did, my boss and I agreed that I shouldn't tell my staff until the end of the fiscal year. The staff was notoriously bad at keeping secrets, and my departure would be a juicy gossip item. It bothered me to not tell my assistant directors about the change, but I followed my boss's guidance. I later found out that the news had leaked from my boss's staff, but I felt good that I had kept the confidence.

I received another confirmation from God that day that I was on the right track. In my daily quiet time that morning I had read Mark 6:31: "He said to them, 'Come aside by yourselves to a deserted place and rest a while.' For there were many coming and going, and they did not even have time to eat." Even Jesus and the disciples needed time away from the rat race of their day? Sounded like it to me. The words jumped off the page as I read them.

My mind was still filled with worry about my physical condition and my attacks, but the knowledge that I would soon be coming away with Christ gave me courage to make it through the month of September and the craziest part of the fiscal year. Somehow God would help me stay afloat. He surely would help me find peace when I made it to October 9—my D-day for leaving work.

Thankfully, as the days ticked down, my anxiety attacks subsided with only a few minor exceptions. My increasing calm was like that of a man who has been floating for days on a raft in the ocean but could see the Coast Guard cutter coming toward him. I was still adrift, but salvation was on its way. Besides, the big sharks were scared off by the approaching cutter.

Continuing Confirmation

God continued to confirm my plans through my daily life at work. After a grueling two-hour commute one Tuesday morning, I showed up in the office worn out before the day had even started.

"You look terrible," Marsha said. "You're so late. I got your text, but the big guy upstairs is grumbling for his reports, and I don't know how to retrieve the information for Benjamin's group."

"No worries, I'm here now." In a few moments, my computer came to life, and the reports were printed. At this busy time of year, everyone wanted to track expenditures closely to make sure we were meeting our goals.

Suddenly I heard a scream in the next office, then, "Jesus, take me back to the Air Force!" The office next to mine was inhabited by two of my employees. I leapt up to see what was the matter.

Somewhat to my horror, I saw Vermeil standing near her desk with her chair toppled over behind her. Her leg was covered in the blood and guts of a deceased rodent.

"I'm so sorry, Vermeil. Let me get you some paper towels," I offered sympathetically.

"No, that's okay. I'll just head to the ladies' room. Then I'm going home for the day."

"I understand," I said, though I really didn't. Well, I understood Vermeil's feelings but not the incident itself. How could this modern-looking building have rats? And why would the maintenance people set a trap inches from where this employee put her feet? I didn't understand. My blood pressure elevated a bit with this incident.

Remembering—and Anticipating—Childlike Joy

As the office noises hummed loudly outside my door, I noticed a favorite photo on my wall. Soon I would have to collect all these mementoes of my life and put them in a box. No trace of me would remain in this office in a couple weeks.

The picture was of a much younger and more fit version of me when I had led a group of ten guys on a ministry trip to West Virginia to go whitewater rafting.

We had arrived at the river in three different cars about dusk. We had set up our tents and then gone to dinner as a group. It was so much fun getting to know these friends better.

In the morning we rose early and headed to the river. Part of the "fun" was carrying our eight-man rafts as a group down to the water's edge. We put in to the river and began our seven-hour trip down the whitewater. At some points along the way we got out of the boat and dove off rocks and jumped into sink holes—activities most of us would have eschewed under normal circumstances. The fact that the danger was controlled made it fun. The group dynamic made the stunts irresistible. While some risk was involved, we felt safe because literally thousands of others had survived the same river antics.

We went over one set of rapids with nearly a twenty-foot drop-off, and our beefy guide popped off the back of the boat. Later we swam alongside the raft and enjoyed a host of adventures that totally wore us out.

After dinner that night we went to a movie to cap off our fun time together. On the drive back the next morning, my passenger and I fought hard to stay awake for the six-hour journey. When I got home, I headed to the loveseat for an afternoon of sleeping and then went to bed for the night. The next day, I felt like a new person. Any feelings of worry I'd had before the trip had been completely erased by the fun and physical exhaustion of it all.

As I sat gazing at the photo on my office wall, I remembered a moment from the trip with my friend, Pat. He had been having fun swimming and playing on the rocks and joking with our guide, and when he looked at me and smiled, his face looked ten years younger than I'd ever seen him look. The childlike enjoyment of playing on the river for a day had lifted all the cares of Washington life.

Sometimes I wondered if I could gather all the sad people in a van and take them to Disney World for a day so we could run and laugh and play with all our hearts. Too many people in the business world never looked as if they were having fun; their faces were drawn, and they often looked as if they'd lost their best friend. I knew that I looked this way too some days. But not so much now with my sabbatical in sight.

Looking for My Happy Place

As I listened to others in the office rush to finish their final orders before the fiscal year ended, I felt like a free bird. What was all the fuss about? I decided to do a pre-sabbatical inventory. I wanted to document where I was right now as I embarked on this change in my life.

Putting pen to paper forced me to think about my main reasons for taking a sabbatical and how I hoped to address those matters. As I pondered these things, I came up with what I called the "big four": I wanted to find healing in the physical, emotional, spiritual, and financial aspects of my life. Just for fun, I threw in a bonus reason for a sabbatical: achieving some unfulfilled dreams. Little did I know what God had in store to make one of my biggest life dreams a reality during and after the sabbatical. I began to record my current status on these areas:

Physical. My health problems are a major reason for my taking a sabbatical. I recently slipped down to the nurse's station to capture my weight and have her take my blood pressure. It was high, as usual, even with all the medications I take. But two physical factors in particular influenced my decision to take a sabbatical.

First, being diagnosed with diabetes just after starting here at the agency has been a shocking wakeup call. Too many years of carrying too many pounds took a toll on my health. My top weight, before I started the "Losing to Live" program at church, was 330 pounds. (I've lost sixty pounds so far, but I still have a long way to go.) This led to my thrombosed hemorrhoid and the scary news from my doctor that my blood-sugar level was above two hundred (normal is one hundred.) Having known several people who have died of diabetes, it is obvious that I need major lifestyle changes to avoid some nasty consequences of this disease.

Second, the sudden escalation of my lifelong fear of high places and the strange feeling that I am about to have a heart attack or something worse has been quite disturbing. Although this sounds like a mental problem, I feel some kind of chemical change in my body right before the attacks. It feels physiological. Does that make me crazy? I hope to find answers and relief during my sabbatical.

Emotional. Emotional factors were the one area where a sabbatical was not really needed to fix problems. As a sanguine type, I am often happy just to be with people. Quitting my job to be home alone was not going to be better than seeing friendly faces at work every day. Of course, all the faces weren't friendly, but many were. Bosses often add to the pressures of life because they bring discipline to our work efforts, correction for our mistakes and judgement about our results. The mere sound of their voice on the phone can cause pressure. However, co-workers and employees tended to make me feel happy. Just because of the way I was wired mentally, all the people at work (even bosses) were fascinating to me. Their unique ways of expressing themselves, solving problems or reacting to situations fed emotional needs in me.

As the sabbatical approached, I was not sad or depressed. But I was not feeling like myself. I felt a lot of angst about my future with God and the meaning of life. Without time to stop and rest, it is hard for me to say where these feelings may go. I knew that there was much that is right about my life and that I had many things I don't want to lose. However, I also experienced feelings of helplessness and certainly many fears that needed to be addressed. By taking time away, I hoped to reconnect with my dreams, hopes, and ambitions.

I felt a deadening as I entered my fifties. It was as if the things that once gave me so much pleasure hardly mattered anymore. I've always been an avid Ohio State football fan, and I like pro football too, But suddenly the games didn't seem to matter very much.

Spiritual. While I had substantial and obvious problems in the physical and some in the emotional areas of my life, I will begin my sabbatical feeling relatively close to God. I probably couldn't do the sabbatical without this close relationship. I do also have a bit of a dead feeling, but this has lessened as I have taken the leap of faith to quit my job. I am getting closer to Jesus just by planning this big step. How I long to spend hours reading God's Word and books by people who have written of God's love in their lives. Reading will be a big part of my time away.

I'm sad to admit that, despite my love for God, I also had some fear in my relationship with Him. Respect for God is healthy, but I was experiencing a lack of understanding of all God is and all He wants for my life. By praying into these questions during the sabbatical, I hoped God will take me on His lap and teach me more about Himself.

Financial. To be honest, my finances are definitely not where I would like them to be this close to federal government retirement age. My sabbatical isn't going to fix these issues; however, I hoped to learn what has hindered me financially and how I can improve. Due to the dip in the real-estate market around Washington DC, my plan to flip my house went awry. As a result, I am stuck in a house with an extremely high mortgage payment and other bills to boot. While I am aware of the extent of my problems before my sabbatical, I expect that my journey during and after the sabbatical will help me learn how to whack my spending and increase my earning.

Bonus—unfulfilled dreams. Perhaps the craziest part of my desire to have a sabbatical is my unfilled dream of working in a more creative job than the one in which I currently worked. I have always loved singing, acting and the entertainment industry. I have also always wanted to write a book. The sabbatical will help me identify and successfully explore some of the unfulfilled dreams locked in my heart.

As I had walked through my life, my senses had dulled. I had descended into a gray place in which the future had lost its sense of promise and peace eluded me. Now my sabbatical would enable me to look for a new happier place in my soul. God wanted me to move forward and continue growing. He didn't want me to be satisfied with the same old life and same old things. He had created me to explore and to become happier each day.

Beginning with the realization that happiness had passed me by would motivate me to seek God each day for His joy. He wanted me to be happy, and I was about to find out just how much.

Ready for the Big Change

With only a week left at work, I told my staff that I would be leaving the following Friday. Some were surprised, but all were kind to me. They took it well and commenced planning a nice farewell party for me.

The practical matters in checking out of a big government agency were not few. But all the rituals, put together with packing and attending good-bye parties, helped me adjust mentally and emotionally to the major change that was coming in my life.

My sabbatical formation had looked somewhat like the process of buying a car. What would the entire thing look like for me? What was I buying? How would it feel? What would I enjoy if I selected this make and model? Was this something I needed right now or just wanted? Was I willing to pay the cost to have it? My personal sabbatical plan had gotten some meat on its bones, and I liked what I saw. I was definitely willing to pay the price for it.

I even "test drove" my sabbatical. After mapping out how I wanted to spend each day, I followed the plan on my last Saturday before I left my job. I tried to imagine how I would feel on the first day of the sabbatical. The average sabbatical day felt very good. I was ready to buy.

10

LAST DAY OF WORK, FIRST DAY OF BLISS

OCTOBER 9, 2009. MY LAST DAY OF WORK. Our fiscal year was over, and everyone breathed a giant sigh of relief. My agreed-upon day of departure had been a week away, then two days away. Now it was here.

This natural ending point felt right. It would have been unfair to my employees, associate directors, and bosses for me to have left a month or two earlier. I genuinely cared about my co-workers and hadn't wanted to leave them in a bind. I also hadn't wanted to burn my bridges should I want to return. Although I thought my supervisors liked my work enough that they would want to hire me back in the future, nothing is certain in quitting one's job. It was best for me to leave on good terms. This turned out to be more true than I could have predicted.

My farewell meal at the Old Ebbitt Grill was a lot of fun. My co-workers and I had a great time sharing lunch and reminiscing over the trials and tribulations we'd shared over the last three years. We told stories of the hardships of being understaffed, the several employees who had abandoned ship due to the craziness and the demands of staying late to complete a major acquisition.

The food was delicious and made me think of several luncheons and breakfasts I'd enjoyed at this restaurant. One Christmas I had taken my associate directors to this Washington landmark for brunch. I still had the picture of my smiling staff amid the tasteful, seasonal decorations.

My farewell luncheon went by quickly, and my co-workers hustled me back to the office, since two members of upper management were coming over to our department for a cookie reception. Both managers said some extra nice things about me, as did several of our customers who attended the reception. My boses at the time were very classy in such transitions. In perfect business geek fashion, my co-workers gave me a large poster with a giant graph on it. The graph depicted a major accomplishment in metrics form and was signed by many of my co-workers and staff. As a confirmed metrics geek, I loved the gift.

After the party I made the rounds and said good-bye to the people who meant the most to me. Some of my best memories in my twenty-seven years of government service involved the people I'd worked with over the last three years here at this agency. We joked about the good times and the bad. Before long it would be time for me to leave.

Not knowing for sure when or where I would be working next, I took a few minutes alone in my office to thank God for all the great days He had given me in federal service. This work had not only paid my bills but had given me a chance to be a director and to care for other people. It had made a way for me to improve my faith on the playing field, where it mattered. People often looked at work as drudgery or something to be avoided, but I believed that God gave us work to make us better people, help Him care for His world, and allow us to contribute something of value to our fellow travelers.

By successfully finishing out the fiscal year, I was able to leave in the good graces of my bosses. During the cookie reception, they had thanked me, given me beautiful parting gifts, and even hurried through the presentation of a performance award that I hadn't expected to receive. (I left two months before the time when such awards were normally given out.)

I didn't leave the building until I had transitioned all my work to the acting division director, wiped clean my e-mail account, deleted my computer files, and returned all the government property I'd used, including my cell phone and laptop computers. I wanted to tie up any loose ends to avoid confusion in departure. I also remembered to gather all the contact information I would need for a robust job hunt. All of these steps were like unburdening myself of necessary weights that we carry in our daily lives. The more the day wore on, the lighter I felt.

When the time for me to physically leave came, a junior employee walked me to security and saw me out of the building. Ironically, it was the same employee who had seen me having a panic attack but had thought I was just feeling ill. As we walked toward the revolving door, it felt strange to leave the building knowing that I wouldn't be coming back on Monday. I felt like the man on the life raft stepping up into the Coast Guard rescue boat. Things were going to be different, but they had to be better.

Free

When I walked out the door of that shiny office building for the last time before my sabbatical, I was no longer a federal employee.

This felt very weird. After more than twenty-seven years, I suddenly wasn't something I'd been for a very long time. People get our identity, in part, from our jobs. Yet I wasn't afraid at all. Maybe fear would arrive when my money started running out, but today I was just free. I was one very happy sabbatical guy.

I knew exactly why I was on sabbatical. At fifty years of age, I was convinced that taking time off to understand my life couldn't be put off for even one more day. It was time for me to take inventory of who I was and where I wanted to go. In some respects, I had no choice but to take time off. The fear level in my life had been high and going up. I had to get to the bottom of my fears and vanquish or greatly diminish them. I couldn't take any more steps in the darkness. It was time to connect with the greatest power in the universe and throw myself on His mercy. I knew there were answers, and I wasn't going to find them going a hundred miles an hour in a typical Washington lifestyle.

That evening I wrote down all the reasons for my sabbatical on one page, even though I'd written many pages before. My whole plan was in front of me, and for some reason I believed it was going to work:

- Quit job (done).
- Use Thrift Savings Plan to pay off credit cards and pay bills for six to eight months.
- Eventually rent house if necessary and move in with friend.
- Spend time in prayer.
- Read a bunch of books to explore fears, new ideas for the rest of my life, and reasons for my past failures and success.
- Write a book or two (particularly a book about my sabbatical)
- Take two or three trips.
- Get close to God by exploring the big questions about Him, life, and me.
- Thank and praise God for His many gifts to me, including the sabbatical.

A Wonderful New Day

On Monday morning, October 12, I woke up happy for the first time in a very long time. The adventure fed my soul immediately. I started the day with a light breakfast after having had a full night of sleep. The pre-winter weather was still quite mild in the Washington suburbs, and I opened the windows in the sunroom at the back of my house. Octagon shaped and painted a light smoky blue-gray color, the walls blended well with the clouds above and the darker blue-gray tile below.

My seating choices in this room included a comfortable La-Z-Boy recliner or a loveseat. This morning I draped myself across the loveseat with my head resting on one end and my legs dangling over the other. This was a treasured spot for me to think, pray, and read. It would become more so. Squirrels dashed back forth across the small deck just outside the French doors. The mighty walnut tree towered above. Having a nut-bearing tree above a new sunroom hadn't seemed so smart when the first few nuts had hit the glass of the sunroom ceiling the first time, but eventually I stopped worrying about it, as the nuts didn't seem to hurt the glass.

After a meaty time of reading the Scriptures and prayer, I called a friend who was standing vigil with her ill husband. He had Parkinson's disease and was confined to a nursing home, and I was able to offer her some comfort. At lunch I walked to the home of a friend of mine nearby and ate lunch with him. We consumed gyros and laughed about how I had manned up and quit my job. Walking home, I looked around my neighborhood for the first time in a long time. I began to pray for the people in each house as I walked.

In the afternoon I tackled the first book on my reading list, *Believe That You Can* by Jentezen Franklin. It was a wonderful book, filled with encouragement and hope. Soon reading dissolved into a delicious nap. It was exquisite to wake up with the fall air wafting in and realize that I hadn't napped in years. My body, soul, and mind quickly adapted to rest mode.

When a person is very tired, it is natural simply to rest. Why hadn't I seen this while I was working? It seemed so effortless on day one of the sabbatical.

My accomplishments for the day included several things:

- Wrote three pages for a book project.
- Comforted my friend by phone.
- Fixed a buddy's car that wouldn't start.
- Moved pavers from the bottom of the yard up the hill to the top (been meaning to do that for a couple of years).
- Laughed.
- Wrote to two friends on Facebook.
- Ate a little too much.

I also heard from God through Jentezen Franklin's book. First, I discovered, there are four barriers to dreams: lack, limitation, hindrance, and a devourer. Second, we must enter the faith zone by believing God and praising Him even when we have only the partial answer. Third, we should do what is right, despite our fears. And fourth, someday I would own or work at a retreat center where helping stressed out people would be a vocation.

11

TAKING INVENTORY

I SPENT THE FIRST MONTH or so of my sabbatical doing two things: slowing down and taking inventory of my life. I lay on the loveseat in my sunroom a lot and read, thought, and prayed.

Thanks to the age in which we live, I had many great books, movies, websites, audio recordings, and countless other means of learning new things. I was thankful that so many people who had been given wisdom from God had taken time to write down their lessons so that I could learn from them.

It was reading that taught me that I should take an inventory periodically. I noticed that some people took inventory of their lives by concentrating on the sins they'd committed; others looked at good things they'd done; others compared their accomplishments to those of other people. None of these methods seemed productive to me. I wanted to look at the facts about myself at age fifty and bring these facts to God in prayer, in Scripture reading, and in consultation with those who seemed to know more about the subjects surrounding my life than I did. These ideas turned into conversations as I scheduled lunch approximately once a week with one friend, pastor or former co-worker. For me, thinking is sometimes a collaborative venture and the sabbatical gave me time to collaborate.

I took inventory on my big four reasons for taking a sabbatical: physical, emotional, spiritual, and financial needs. In the physical arena, I looked at my weight, anxiety attacks, eating habits, and physical activity. When it came to emotional needs, I decided that I should do two or three activities to maintain social contact. As I documented my perceived spiritual issues or shortcomings, I considered current disciplines that could fix the issues and proposed new activities or actions to work on. Finally, I took an accounting of my financial activities, past mistakes, and current budget and planned to learn two or three things that I could do differently to improve my financial health. By looking over these four areas at the beginning of my sabbatical, I got some clues as to which issues needed to be addressed in my prayer time, reading, counseling with friends or pastors, and activities.

From this evaluation I realized that I needed some major help regarding finances, my physical health, and what I referred to as "the fear problem." My desire to fix these issues informed my reading list and led me to certain books that addressed these matters specifically.

Getting Down to Business

My inventory began with my attacks. I tried to understand my fears and place them alongside God's truth. At first no illumination came. My fears and I coexisted for the first month of my sabbatical. Bringing them to the fore only seemed to induce more fear.

As I sought God, however, He sent brothers and sisters to pray with me, talk with me, and extend grace to me. This illustrated for me the scripture, "Grace be to you and peace from God our Father, and from the Lord Jesus Christ" (2 Cor. 1:2). Fellowship with my brothers and sisters in Christ literally brought God's grace to me when I needed it. I hadn't known it, but I needed their prayers and their physical representation of His grace before I was ready to learn. For the time being I simply rested in their fellowship and examined other areas of my life.

Finances became a major focus in those early days of my time off. This was an area in which I needed learning and discipline. My sabbatical gave me an amazing opportunity to recalibrate my finances and start planning for the end game of my retirement. This seemed especially important in light of the fact that I had raided my Thrift Savings Plan to finance the sabbatical.

I began reading Dave Ramsey's book *Total Money Makeover*. After that I read all the Dave Ramsey books I could find, and his teaching helped me take inventory of my financial picture. The result was bleak, particularly for someone my age.

A couple days after totaling up my debts, I got the courage to look into my credit scores. I hadn't expected soaring numbers, but I was disappointed to find my scores lower than I'd hoped. *Whoa! How did I get these numbers?* I wondered. My only real blemish had been letting my home loan go thirty-one days in arrears. However, I'd paid the loan current with the last check from my job, which had included my regular salary for two weeks and a performance bonus of a few thousand dollars.

My financial inventory made it clear to me that I'd been living a lie. For years I had pretended that I could spend without fetters and expect no consequences. I'd been bailed out twice before by selling fixer-upper houses; the first time I'd made about a hundred and fifteen thousand and the second time two hundred thousand. Each time I'd paid off all my bills, given a hefty chunk to church and other charities, and paid the down payment on the next fixer upper. Unfortunately, I had bought my current house at the top of the market, and housing values had plummeted shortly afterward. It would be a long time before I would see any of the money from my ninety-thousand-dollar down payment, if ever.

Dave Ramsey recommended a definite course of action for a person in my situation. His "baby steps" to recovery became my financial bible.

Of all the gifts that the sabbatical gave me, one of the best was helping me understand my finances in light of my personality. It gave me the opportunity and the means of turning my financial life over to God. My best thinking had left me far in debt and within inches of falling off a cliff. With God's help I was able begin rebuilding this part of my life. Getting off the treadmill of life allowed me to wake up and figure out what had to be done if I was to have any hope of a financially secure retirement.

Throughout my sabbatical I saw many financial miracles. I also learned the practical disciplines of budgeting more carefully and projecting cash flow better. God provided everything I needed at just the right time. If I had received up front the large sum that I eventually received from the retirement fund, I may have spent on the wrong things and not had enough to last through my sabbatical.

The biggest financial miracle involved a payment for my unused vacation time. After I got my mortgage current and paid other bills at the beginning of the sabbatical, I was running short of funds. Just when I needed money to buy groceries, a check for unused vacation time arrived. It was valued at more than nine thousand dollars. This brought me through the first difficult time of the sabbatical and let me focus on other things besides money.

As I prayed for guidance about my finances, I learned four things that God didn't want me going into to debt for: eating out, missionary's hotel rooms (don't ask), cars, and daily needs such as groceries and gas. I had to learn to live on what I was making. Like needing to put on one's own oxygen mask before putting on the mask of a child, I needed to get my own finances straight before trying to bail out relatives and friends. I couldn't give beyond what God was asking or treat large groups at a restaurant after church.

During the sabbatical I also read *The Blessed Life*, a great book by Robert Morris. The way he explained the importance of living below our means to enable us to give to others hit home with me. I loved to give to other people. My fault was that I wasn't living far enough below my means to enable me to give. God does occasionally test us to see if we will give when we can't afford it. I, however, had literally tithed myself into a "very poor" credit rating. On the one hand, I was following God's Word by tithing. On the other hand, I was disobeying another part of His Word that said that the borrower becomes a slave to the lender (see Proverbs 22:7).

Besides starting to examine my anxiety attacks and straightening out my finances, I also worked on a physical health plan and began to spend great amounts of time with the Lord, thinking and praying and reading His Word.

A New Routine

All this led to a revised schedule for an average sabbatical day.

I started every day after a full night of sleeping eight hours. (This took away any guilt about going to bed late but kept some level of discipline in my life.) Then it was "shower, shave, Aqua Velva," as I liked to describe my morning routine. It felt great to enjoy the new bathroom I had put in a couple years earlier. That tile really was great! The multiple shower jets and smooth rocks on the floor of the shower really woke me. I put on fresh clothes and thanked God for another day.

Next I had devotions. I liked to read the Bible straight without any other text for about twenty or thirty minutes. Then I prayed for family members and friends. I also took several minutes to thank my Creator for all He had done the day before. His hand was everywhere in my life, and I took time to acknowledge it. Then, it was time for small breakfast of cereal or boiled eggs. I seldom woke up hungry, so I stayed with what I'd been eating when I worked.

Then I read one of the books of interest that I had purchased for its special significance to the goals of my sabbatical. (My entire booklist from the sabbatical is printed at the back of this book.) Providentially, a friend had given me Jentezen Franklin's book *Fear Fighters*. Since fear was a problem for me, I enjoyed every word of this helpful text.

Next I usually began doing the "work" of my sabbatical. This included either studying a facet of my life or helping a friend write his book.

For lunch each day I made a simple meal, and a friend of mine who lived just a few blocks away and worked only part time often came by to share stories and talk about his book, also under development. His great companionship provided an outlet for some of my ideas, and it was fun to hear his reactions to my thoughts.

After lunch I tried to get out of the house. Sometimes this meant going to the gym. Other days I might browse used bookstores in the neighborhood or go to the supermarket. It was amazing to spend extra time driving to a supermarket a few miles away just to get fresher vegetables at a discount price. When I was working, I always jammed grocery shopping into the few available minutes I had. Now it was a luxury to shop well and eat healthy foods.

When I returned home in the afternoon, I read my book of the moment again. This often led to a nap. What a fascinating thing—to nap in the middle of the afternoon! This persisted through the first two or three months of the sabbatical until I was literally all rested up and no longer needed naps. For one of the first times in the past twenty years or so, I felt completely rested. My mind worked better. Memory increased. Mood lightened. Comprehension quickened.

My brain started to perform at a higher level than before the sabbatical. I felt twenty years younger.

Supper was often at a restaurant with friends, or I had someone over for dinner.

Most of the time the evenings were about television and relaxing before bed. Sometimes I did this with friends and sometimes by myself. It was so peaceful not to worry about getting to bed in order to be up at five forty-five so I could get to work downtown. I also went out to concerts and movies during the evenings.

Worship, Fellowship, and Reflection

Sundays now took on new meaning. Instead of thinking about errands I needed to run or laundry that must be started as soon as I returned from church, I relaxed and just concentrated on Jesus. My obligations as an elder were gone.

My worship took on new meaning, and I started going to church an hour early for a teaching series. I put the focus on Jesus. Worship came up from inside me—as God intended it should do. The stale feeling I'd had before the sabbatical left.

After the church service I spent time with other church members instead of hurrying home. This renewed interest in fellowship led me to understand my own issues better. God led me to other people who had been through anxiety or faced hindrances to their walk with Him. By taking time for lunch with them after church, my spirit was renewed in Christian fellowship. I began to rest in my relationships in a new way. When two or more got together with Jesus on their minds, amazing miracles happened. I couldn't begin to tell of all the good ideas, reassurance, and peace that came to me through Christian fellowship during this time. I like to think that I helped them as well.

In these early days of my sabbatical, while I adjusted to a slower pace of life and allowed myself to think through my needs, I identified several critical issues in my life:

1. What was I supposed to be doing with my life? This question led to several others, including: why was I put here on Earth? Was God really in control of when I would die? Did I have anything to fear if God was on my side?

2. Were all the great times of my life behind me? (This question was common to people in middle life—age forty to sixty.) I was blessed to have done many fun and worthwhile things in my life, but from everything I'd seen of my friends' lives, a lot of things went downhill from age fifty. What could I do to ensure that the rest of my days would be as rewarding and fun as my first fifty years?

3. Was there a way I could help a lot of people and thereby live up to the potential that I'd seen in myself in years past?

These questions and a lot of free time led to the spiritual journey at the heart of my sabbatical:

- What barriers had kept me from being who I should be?
- What were my fears, and how could I be relieved of them?
- Did I have any addictions? Idols? Fatal flaws?
- Did I have any deep hurts? How could they be healed?
- How had I sinned against others?
- What was the way of forgiveness for me and for others?
- How could I live a resurrected life?

As I settled into my sabbatical, I was surprised at how easy it was to accept that I'd quit my job. Doing so had been a necessary bridge to my tomorrow, and I felt complete peace that God had led me to this place of rest and communion with Him. While I missed the hustle and bustle of being busy and the interaction with friends, it was also easy to step away. Being alone with God and focused on my critical issues was exactly where I needed to be.

12

FACING MY FEAR

ONE MORNING EARLY IN MY SABBATICAL, I lay down on the loveseat in my sunroom and looked up at the sky. The tinted glass in the roof made everything a little bluer than normal. The clouds were fluffy white with just a hint of blue, but the sky was fabulously blue.

I stared toward the heavens and watched the clouds move across the sky. Suddenly my mind started to play tricks on me. I felt the rotation of the earth, and it made me fearful. What if it didn't rotate right? *Now that's reaching for things to be fearful about,* I thought. Illogical fear gripped me until I stopped looking up. Here was my peaceful haven, and I was migrating toward a panic attack.

"Oh, Lord," I cried out. "How can I be going so nuts so young? What is wrong with me? But even if I go all the way nuts, even if I have a heart attack from the fear, I'm going to lie here and look at that beautiful sky." The desperation in my voice reminded me of why I was no longer working and instead lying on a loveseat at ten in the morning on a weekday.

Just as a person needs a solid car, boat, or plane under him before embarking on a physical journey, having honesty at the core of my spiritual journey was vital. It was just God and me now. I had no reason to lie or even kid myself. No reason to pretend that things were better than they seemed. God knew everything about me and loved me unconditionally.

As I calmed down, I picked up Jentezen Franklin's book *Fear Fighters*. If I didn't know anything else, I was sure that I had to find solutions to my fear problem during my sabbatical. Although I hadn't received any distinct answers the first month or so, I knew that at some point I needed a solution to these relatively new unwanted visitors to my life: panic attacks. Whether my fears were caused by a chemical imbalance, a spiritual problem, or habitual worrying, I needed to let God into this part of my life.

The fix needed to go beyond the Band-Aids I had used for coping. The Ativan and other pills that my doctor had prescribed for my sudden panic problems had helped at times in the past, but they didn't help long term. Some friends of mine even wondered if the medication actually made things worse. For the permanent improvement I needed, taking a walk around the block or popping an Ativan wasn't going to cut the mustard. I needed answers, and I needed God to provide them.

I didn't know much about Jentezen Franklin except that he was a preacher and teacher who had a television ministry (which I'd never watched up to this point). And I knew that he started each year with fasting and prayer. I respected this, because it indicated to me that he sought God's help for the challenges he would face each year. As I turned the pages of his book, it became obvious to me that he had heard from the Holy Spirit while he was writing. So much wisdom—and the words began to heal my mind. It wasn't an instantaneous thing, but day by day on the loveseat in my sunroom, I began to get a picture of the freedom that was available to me.

Having been a Christian since the age of twelve, I knew that Jesus was my Savior. I had prayed, and He had forgiven me for my sin. I had been baptized, and I continued to seek God now. But even though I was washed in the blood and heading for heaven, I had known a lot of fear and anxiety in my life. Some Christians had offered quick fixes for my fears. They had prayed, and I had sincerely believed God to answer their prayers. But my fears didn't go away—not for long, at least.

As I began to learn from Franklin's book and then from *Fearless* by Max Lucado, I pressed in with God through prayer. I felt that God wanted me to explore my fears with His Word and with brothers who were more mature than me as my guides. Both books taught me things I hadn't known and hadn't had time to learn before the sabbatical. Jentezen Franklin helped me understand God's plan for my reassurance. Max Lucado examined in detail several of people's most common fears, including the fear of death. This began the process of releasing me from bondage.

Changing Things Up

While my anxiety issues must have stemmed in part from spiritual matters and deeply held beliefs, they were also affected by my physical health, or lack thereof. As I reviewed my physical condition, I saw that it was not great. While I'd lost sixty pounds before starting the sabbatical through the Losing to Live program, I still tipped the scales at 270 or so, and no health guide recommends this weight for longevity! Weight wasn't the only gauge of my health, but all my other indicators agreed with the scale. For me there are a lot of mental gymnastics to weight loss, but I have to seek honesty.

I had to laugh at a corpulently obese woman I saw on a talk show. She was advocating for how incredibly healthy she was at five foot two and 260 pounds. She claimed that she regularly walked up two flights of stairs at work and did all her own housework. Really? Was her heavy breathing as she sat stationary in the studio an indicator of her health? She reminded me of me, except that I didn't have any delusion about being healthy.

Yes, I occasionally worked out. Yes, I took a mangosteen-based super antioxidant vitamin called Vemma. However, neither of these counteracted overeating and under-exercising.

The inventory of my health issues wasn't long, but neither was it pretty:

- Have high blood pressure—sort of controlled through medication
- Have diabetes—on a pill for that
- Huff and puff when climbing stairs or bending over to tie shoes
- Generally feel yucky quite often
- Have periodic anxiety attacks

In short, I had plenty of room for improvement in my physical health. Thanks to Pastor Steve Reynold's Losing to Live program, I knew many of the right things to do to continue losing weight. Steve Reynolds and his weight-loss competition had kept me motivated and eager to continue learning more about health.[1] To meet my fellowship needs and ensure that I had a team to help me lose weight, I continued to participate in the Losing to Live program at church. It was great fun watching others also lose weight and hearing their ideas for shedding pounds.

Pastor Reynold's book *Bod 4 God* was indispensable in my physical recovery. *Bod 4 God* taught me to eat less. While working I had often taken shortcuts that blunted my success in losing weight. For example, I shopped at the market on Sunday and bought four or five healthy entrees for dinners. Then pressing matters at work caused me to leave an hour later than usual. Starving, I stopped by a fast-food restaurant and grabbed a six-hundred-calorie burger and a four-hundred-calorie order of fries. When I finally made it home, my favorite chair called, and I was done thinking about health for the evening. The sabbatical gave me a chance to rewire my eating habits. This included ditching my habit of drinking large amounts of Diet Pepsi.

Shopping for food during the sabbatical was more than fun. Instead of rushing to the store after church each Sunday and before doing chores around the house, I used my daily afternoon breaks to drive to a store several miles away that had a great fresh-vegetable selection. This store not only had great produce, but it charged less than the bigger stores in my neighborhood. Farmer's markets were later added to my rotation after I returned to work.

The sabbatical also gave me time to look up healthy recipes and create new soups. One of my favorites was chili barley chicken. It included asparagus, onion, a packet of McCormick's chili, diced tomatoes, kidney beans, chicken breast, water, and pearled barley. I put the mixture in the Crock-Pot after breakfast and enjoyed it with friends at dinner time.

Bod 4 God also taught me to exercise more. I found that a neighboring town had an older YMCA with affordable rates; joining with a friend further reduced the price. The gym included several pools and an amazing circuit-training room that used a technology called FitLinxx. When I used a sign-in code, FitLinxx tracked my settings and accomplishments at each weight-lifting machine. It also allowed me to record my cardio activities like riding a stationary bike, using an elliptical trainer, or swimming. Following each workout FitLinxx provided many metrics, including total weight lifted and weight stations visited, and it awarded points, which helped feed my competitive side.

By changing up my workout routine, I was able to make substantial strength gains and also reconnect with my love of swimming.

My biggest lifestyle change was beginning to walk around my neighborhood. The walks helped me recharge after hours of reading or praying. I really enjoyed the nature I discovered in the blocks surrounding my suburban home. I saw deer, rabbits, rats (ugh!), geese, cardinals, an extremely malnourished fox, raccoons, and even a horse that was bound for some parade.

Trying Something New

On one of my early sabbatical mornings, I prayed for God to show me anything I needed to know to stop the anxiety attacks. I had been convinced for a long time that a physical component existed in these episodes, so when I visited my family doctor for an annual physical just a few days later, I went hoping that God would give me some answers.

Up to this point my doctor had found little reason to explain my physical condition, only speculating that perhaps my blood-sugar levels or my potassium were a bit low. He had declared my episodes to be simple panic attacks.

Although this visit was a regular physical just to cover the basics, I opened up to my doctor about the anxiety attacks. Rather than having him add another pill to my regimen, I spontaneously asked if I could stop taking Actos, which I'd been taking for diabetes. Actos had been the last pill added to my regimen, I reasoned, and perhaps it wasn't interacting well with my blood-pressure medication or my unique body chemistry. My doctor agreed, but he said that I would need to go back on some kind of medication if my sugar numbers increased. I had no idea if quitting Actos would make any difference at all, but it was definitely worth a try.

Fear on Broadway

That weekend I took the train to New York City with a good buddy of mine for a short vacation. One of my favorite things was to catch Broadway shows and eat out at New York restaurants.

For a small-town Ohio boy, the glamour of New York and Broadway was great fun, and the creativity of some of those shows was amazing. The two-night trip would include three shows, some eating out, and general sightseeing.

Overall we had a fun time, but fear raised its ugly head between the fun times. The large buildings of Midtown Manhattan near our hotel stressed me out. I didn't plan on going into them, but the very sight of these skyscrapers made me feel queasy and anxious. This visit to New York wasn't ruined by my anxiety, but my worry was sizable. I tried to pray and turn my fears over to God, but it didn't work. As my friend and I walked down the street, I could barely talk. Though I tried to cover up my phobias, my friend noticed that something was wrong.

That first evening after our arrival, I asked God to show me what was going on. As it turned out, God wanted to use this experience as a field trip in my healing.

We went to see the Broadway show *Promises, Promises* starring Kristin Chenoweth. I absolutely loved this singer and actress; she had an incredible voice and totally captivated me. I had great tickets down front. We made our way to the very first row, right next to the sunken orchestra pit.

But as my friend and I sat down, my palms became sweaty. The drop-off between our seats and the stage frightened me. My face became flushed, and I grew angry at myself. What would I tell my friend? Was I too nuts to even take in a show now? I prayed and tried to focus on the music and acting going on just a few feet beyond the orchestra pit.

As the show began, I tried to settle in and relax. The sets were beautiful, the Burt Bacharach music was sublime, and the singing and acting were terrific. But finally I made up a fake illness and told my friend that I needed to go to the restroom. I figured that I could then stand at the back of the theater until I felt better. What actually happened was that the usher reseated me near the back of the auditorium, and I enjoyed the rest of the show from there. Afterward I made excuses to my friend, and we headed back to the hotel.

On the train ride home, I prayed fervently that God would help me overcome this crippling panic.

13

FINDING ANSWERS

THE FOLLOWING MONDAY I was back on the loveseat in my sunroom. But as I poured my heart out to God that morning, I began to feel an intimacy with Him like I hadn't before. It was as strong as two lovers feel at the beginning of a relationship. Somehow I knew that He had heard my prayers and was going to take me on a journey with Him to heal me of my fears.

I hadn't experienced such direct communication with God in at least ten years. He knew that I was hurting, and He responded to my seeking by comforting me with the presence of His Spirit. The Scripture and my other books helped me that morning as I prayed through my fears and worries. Faith began to build.

Later in the day I walked around my neighborhood as a break from reading. Prayer came easily as I walked up and down the hilly streets. As I passed by each house, I prayed for the people inside. I knew some of my neighbors, but most were represented only by a certain kind of car, their front-porch decorations, or toddler toys in the yard. I'd often found it interesting to imagine all the people living in those houses. They all had lives—some of them happy, some distraught, most in between. They were young or old, addicted or sober, and God knew and loved every one of them.

During these precious prayer times that I continued in the following days, I sensed that God was changing our neighborhood. It was as if the spiritual DNA of our community began to heal just a little as I walked and prayed. This was not because I personally had any power to change these people by praying but because God chooses to work through the prayers of His children.

About a week after discontinuing the Actos, I began to feel better. My anxiety lessened. Whether from quitting the diabetes drug or giving up Diet Pepsi or reading Jentezen Franklin and Max Lucado, I felt much better. It was remarkable to have this horrible, crippling illness begin to diminish so suddenly. I still had no desire to ride the elevator to the top of the Empire State Building, but I was incredibly hopeful as I realized the fear might just be losing its grip.

Fear and Christians

Fear, I reflected and prayed through these matters, was definitely one of the most destructive forces for Christians.

When I was growing up, my family was Methodist. Our belief system, as I understood it, was that we came to church, heard good stuff from the Bible, thought it through, and worked together to help each other and the community. The minister we had for most of my youth had been told some goofy things in seminary, and his liberal philosophy seemed to teach that if we lived good, moral lives, everything would be all right. I vividly remember a sermon in which he said that if we maintained a good state of mind here on Earth, we would go to a good state of mind when we died. Later, he was replaced by more spiritual men at that church,

But this minister didn't want anyone to make waves at church. He feared that too much truth could drive away parishioners, and how could our church help people if they left and didn't come back? He seemed to reject any real move of the Holy Spirit if anyone at all objected. At one point, several of our youth professed to being born again after attending youth camp, and our pastor attempted to downplay these conversions because they made some of the older parishioners feel nervous. His fear prevented the Spirit from operating fully in our congregation. Some of us eventually left as a result of these and other attempts to reject a faith that occasionally turned emotional.

I thought then about the Fundamentalist church I had attended after the Methodist church. Many of its teachings were Bible based and theologically sound. The people there had a zeal for God that had been missing from my earlier experiences, and this taught me something about the differences between Christians. But there were also some similarities. The Fundamentalists, like the Methodists, had problems with fear—it just showed up in a different way. For some in the congregation, the devil seemed more of a force in their lives than God was. They worried that the devil would make them sick, lead their children astray, or even steal their salvation. In retrospect, I don't believe that God was honored by this lack of faith in Him. Fear can't be our primary motivation for serving God or for how we live our lives. It also can't drive us to doubt God's authentic moves around us just because fear is aroused in those not attuned to the Holy Spirit.

My interactions with normal human Christians had left some scars in my life and sometimes confused my personal theology. It took me a while to discover that it really didn't matter so much what a church believed—what mattered was what I knew about Jesus.

Daily Harassments

It wasn't just issues in the church that had caused me to be afraid. In a world cursed by sin, the devolving of our planet gave me plenty of reasons to worry.

The polar ice caps were melting at a record pace. The world economy was melting down faster than the polar ice caps. Polar bears were headed for extinction, and how far behind them could large, bear-like men be on the endangered list? Such men (like myself) ate a lot and needed hundreds of miles of grazing fields, or at least a Safeway grocery store nearby. And if the world economy went in the toilet, how would Starbucks survive the cataclysm?

If that wasn't enough to worry about, I was disturbed about the inconsiderate ways people treated each other. One day when I was in line at the pharmacy, where the inexperienced staff always mixed up my prescription medications, this woman tried to cut in front of everyone in line. Another customer questioned her integrity, her lineage, and her eyesight before the clerk intervened.

"This lady has been here for over an hour," the clerk cut me off mid tirade. "We had to have her medication sent over from another pharmacy. Besides, she can barely stand with that walker."

"I'm sorry," I sheepishly told the clerk and the lady.

Even I sometimes treated people less than acceptably. Part of it was motivated by fear of being treated unfairly. How can they take this woman ahead of me? Or how can they take so long with her when all of us are waiting? The root fear that they will take so long with her that the store will close or that I won't get my medication is absurd. The store is open 24 hours. Truthfully, it was a solvable problem with just a cup of patience and kindness added to my thoughts before I spoke. Too bad I had been out of patience and kindness that day. Should have looked in Aisle 7.

Sometimes even when I tried to live at peace with everyone, as the Bible instructed Christians to do, things happened that sent me into turmoil.

But this was because a spiritual battle was going on. The forces of evil were trying to win the day, and occasionally they caused upsets that were not of my making. But sometimes these upsets were actually for my good. They let me know that something wasn't right and that I needed to get alone with God and His Word to sort things out. This disquieting of my world could let me know that it was time for a major change in my life.

This was exactly why I was on sabbatical. And the good news was that after a little while, I believed that God would bring me peace again. As I got on my knees before Him, peace would come to my soul, even in the most difficult circumstances. All would be well with my soul. Everything was going to be okay—if I grabbed hold of the hem of Jesus' garments.

Conquering My Fear of Death

It was Max Lucado who helped me conquer, or at least cage, many of my deepest fears. In his book *Fearless* Lucado's words were comforting and nurturing while encouraging manageable steps toward wholeness. His discussion of many common fears devastated me in its loving effect. It made me know that I had to do better, be better, and build my relationship with God.

Perhaps none of Lucado's thoughts on fear helped me more than his look at death. I could face death at any time, whether my own or that of a loved one. How I dealt with the subject of death would inform every other area of my life.

As I looked at fear through the eyes of both Lucado and Franklin, I quickly saw that many of my fears involved death at their core. Knowing that fear was a lack of faith, I wondered about my faith in God to save me completely. Was my real fear that somehow I wouldn't go to heaven when I died? This was a key fact of my Christian life. I had accepted Christ and knew that I was going to spend eternity with Him, but knowing it in my head was different from feeling it in my heart.

So much of my life had been spoiled by thoughts of life's imper-manence, but I knew that death didn't really spell the end of life. When my earthly body lay down and died, my soul would be released to its eternal keeper, and I would spend eternity with Christ and His followers. What could I fear when I knew that my eternal existence was safely in the hands of an everlasting God? How could I worry about tomorrow? These healing thoughts began to penetrate my heart.

As I explored this universal fear of death with my Father in heaven, I came to understand several things on a heart level that I had not previously accepted:

1. Physical dying was a temporary condition that led to eter-nal union with God. I did not need to dread dying. When I died, I would be in the arms of God, as I was now.

2. It was natural and normal to want to avoid death. Dying was unnatural and not what God intended for us. The fall of man brought death into our lives. We were supposed to want to live, so it was okay for me to be repulsed by death.

3. God would do whatever was necessary to help me have the courage needed for each day. He would also grant me the courage I needed to face death when it was my turn to do so.

4. Being a control freak set one up to go nuts about death. No one could ultimately control death. This was one more area in which I needed to relinquish any illusion of control to the One who really did have control: God.

5. Those who wanted to hold onto the notion that a loving God wouldn't send anyone to an eternity in torment should check out Revelation 14:11: "The smoke of their torment ascendeth up forever and ever: and they have no rest day nor night, who worship the beast and his image, and whosoever receiveth the mark of his name." Eternal torment is a real thing, and people need to avoid it at all costs. It was interesting to me to note that one of the hallmarks of hell was that there is no rest there.

Death was not the big ending. For the Christian, death was the gateway to be with the Lord.

It was like my sister, Susie, had once told me. She had battled health problems for many years and used a C-PAP machine to assist her breathing at night. When I told her of some of my fears, she said, "Do what I do. When I wake up in the morning, I take a few breaths. I look around. I say to myself, *Oh I'm still here. God must want me to be alive another day.* In other words, I don't worry about dying." I didn't have to be afraid to die of my panic attacks or anything else, because if God wanted me on Earth, I would stay right here, and if I died, I would go to be with the Lord Jesus.

At Peace in God's Arms

As I sat on the loveseat in my sunroom, I looked up to the sky and marveled that my anxiety about the earth moving had left. Clouds didn't worry me now. Quiet before my Lord, I looked at a thing that had scared me just a few weeks before. The fear was now gone.

At that moment on that day, I was free of fear. It was a new kind of freedom. I didn't have to hurry my mind past the things that made me anxious, hoping not to become overwhelmed with fearful thoughts and disconcerting physical sensations. I could lie there, perfectly still, and reach up to the heavens. God was holding me. Our globe may have been spinning, but I was held securely in His arms.

14

SCARRED BUT HEALED

SLOWING MY LIFE DOWN inevitably resulted in a lot of thinking. As I addressed the difficult issues in my life, particularly my fear, I was reminded of significant painful events from my past. While these events had wounded me, I had also found healing from them along my journey. My sabbatical allowed me time to pray further into these issues and receive greater revelation and clarity about them as God worked in me. As I pondered my memories, I grew to treasure my scars, because they were a sign of healing in my life. Experience taught me (and probably everyone else too) that every life has pain and many things that don't go right.

Memories of My Dad

The deepest scar in my life came from the death of my father.

For thirty years I worried about my dad's health and dreaded the day he would die. As a child, the sound of his coughing often woke me in the night. Shock waves of fear came over me as I lay in bed, staring at the ceiling. Desperate prayers went up to heaven that God would spare my dad for a while longer. As with most boys when it comes to their dads, my father was an anchor in my life. He was able to fix any problem, repair any breach—and finance any indiscretion.

As a sixteen-year-old, I was driving Dad's big yellow Buick Riviera. A friend and I were about to light up a funny cigarette as the Eagles's song "Take It to the Limit" played on the radio. On the busy two-lane road that led to our little town, we came up behind a car that was doing fifty in a fifty-five zone. I hit the gas and quickly passed the car. Suddenly the red lights of a police cruiser came up quickly behind me. I stowed my unlit joint and pulled to the side of the road. Although my heart was racing, instinct took over, and I turned into Eddie Haskell from *Leave It to Beaver*. "Yes, officer." "No, sir." "Yes, sir." Despite my attempts to appear righteous, the officer was unmoved. He gave me a hefty ticket—my first one.

As I came in the door hours earlier than Dad had expected me, he asked the question I had been dreading: "What happened?" I must have looked plenty scared when I told him that I had gotten a ticket. To my surprise, he took the ticket from me and said, "I'll pay for the first one. The rest are up to you."

His generosity didn't shelter me from all consequences, however. A wise judge insisted that I go to traffic school for four two-hour sessions. This caused me to miss a couple of high-school tennis meets.

Traffic school back then mainly consisted of ninety minutes of deadly boring lectures and extremely gruesome films showing the aftermath of horrible wrecks. The point was clear—speeding led to dire consequences. I took their message to heart and drove much more slowly thereafter. The bigger lesson, though, came from Dad. He loved me unconditionally, no matter what I did wrong.

There was another consequence of my actions. Months later, as I sat in class at our large rural high school, an announcement came over the loud speaker: "The following people report to the principal's office," and they started naming every hood and lawbreaker in the school. It was a rogue's gallery of people voted most likely to do five to ten at Southern Ohio Correctional Institution. The list was alphabetical, and I was horrified to hear my name called near the end of the roster. As if for emphasis, my name was pounded out again at the end. I couldn't believe that I was being called to the principal's office and with such an unholy group of hooligans.

When we arrived, a tough man in a suit invited us to sit down and listen. The principal stood next to this man like a mafia underboss. The suit guy invited us to join the county's summer basketball league. It was an opportunity for us to get off the streets and do something productive over the summer. If we completed six sessions, we got a pair of new basketball shoes.

I almost laughed out loud that they were offering us charity shoes for playing basketball. How sad, really. Didn't they know that my parents would buy me whatever shoes I needed?

My head was swimming. There had to be some mistake. I wasn't like these other guys. How had I gotten on a list with the Future Felons of America? Then I remembered my checkered past—I had gotten a speeding ticket. I believed that God was telling me that a reputation is a terrible thing to waste, so I went home and determined to keep my nose clean.

Several years later, when I was just starting out in my career in Chicago, I was pretty down about finances and the hardships of adjusting to life in the big city. I called Dad and told him my troubles. His immediate reaction was to offer me money.

He was a generous man, but funds weren't what I needed, and I told him so. "I don't want your money, I need you," I said as the tears started. He didn't know what to say, and neither did I, but our relationship was strengthened that day.

Relationships, I reflected, were much more important than money. Part of my service to God was to be available to those He wanted me to love, as my dad had been for me.

Saying Good-Bye

In 1990, when I was thirty years old, Dad's emphysema and heart problems put him in the hospital for what seemed like the twentieth time. My mom was watching over him when I arrived from Washington, where I now lived. I had hoped that my dad would die quickly when the time came; I didn't want to be there, because I wasn't sure I could endure it.

That last week with him was precious in so many ways. At the hospital I was surprised to see him alert enough to greet me and carry on a brief conversation. The whole family gathered around him. As we talked, his sense of humor showed through. "I don't know what you expect me to do," he told us. "I can't die on cue."

Eventually he grabbed me somewhat forcefully, for a guy supposedly on his deathbed. He pulled me down and kissed me. It was beautiful, and it gave me hope that he wasn't going away anytime soon.

Mom decided to go to her house with me for the night and try to get some rest. One of my siblings stayed with him overnight. As we drove through the frozen countryside, Mom broke down. Dad was slipping away, and she knew the end was near. At the same time, she didn't know how much longer she could stand to see his pain. Each breath was difficult for him, and he had endured so much torture. She cried as I drove her past the frozen fields where huge corn stalks had grown just months before. I couldn't help but think that the heyday of our family had passed. The good times were gone, I thought; now it would all be about dying and barren endings.

Throughout that week our family experienced indignities and many awful moments. Early on, though, I found a little chapel in the hospital. The room was softly lit and had about ten padded pews, as in a church. At the front was a cross and bas-relief artwork of Jesus holding a lamb. God showed me during that terrible week how He would hold me closer than Jesus was holding that lamb. There were precious times in that chapel between God and me.

Dad passed away as my sister stood watch one night. Mom and I came back to the hospital with my brother and went into Dad's room. I had to touch Dad's body and know that he was gone. As I touched his forehead, I was struck by how inanimate he was. It was obvious that his life force had gone away and he no longer lived in there.

Wow, it was really over. After twenty-plus years of illness, the emphysema had finally killed him. I felt empty now. After the long week of watching him lapse into a coma and seeing the pain on my mother's face, I was exhausted. So many years had been filled with fear of these moments. In some ways, though, Dad's death was easier to take than the years of dreading it.

God's Healing Power

In the days after my dad's passing, I cried hard. My heart was broken to lose my father, and I suddenly realized that I couldn't talk to him again until I too had taken the journey to the other side.

I asked God how things were different for our family as believers. Didn't we experience the same pain as people who didn't know God? What was the advantage of being Christian if our family members died just the same as unbelievers' did? My Dad was as cold in his coffin as any sinner or any relative of a family steeped in darkness.

God answered me so loudly that it was almost audible. "Didn't you see how strange the light was in the hospital room after he died?" I heard in my mind. "Couldn't you tell that My angels had just been there to take him away? Couldn't you feel the presence in that room?" My eyes were suddenly opened, and I remembered the heavenly presence that had filled the area all around his deathbed.

The strange glow had been comforting that night, but I hadn't known why. Now God showed me that anything that had been in contact with heaven took on a second-hand glow from the experience. Like Moses' shining face when he came down from the mountain after communing with God, so was my dad's hospital room after the angels had come to gather my father's soul.

Although my dad's passing was excruciatingly painful and cut me deeply, God's healing power had come to my rescue. It took me almost a year to feel completely normal again, but I experienced many tender mercies along the way, and I walked away healed from my most dreaded loss. My anchor was gone and things were different from then on, but I had a new anchor and a new way to walk in the world.

A wise woman once told me that the only thing keeping a boy from full manhood is his father. Not until his father passes away does he come into the fullness of being a man. I believe this now.

The great loss hurt me deeply and left a tremendous scar on my life. My foundation was shaken when someone who had been a rock in my life was removed. But God left the scar to remind me that all things heal. As I prayed into my dad's death that had taken place almost twenty years earlier, God reminded me once again that He would always be there to comfort me.

15

HAVING FRIENDS AND
BEING A FRIEND

FIVE WEEKS INTO MY SABBATICAL, a friend and I traveled to Newark, New Jersey, for a concert. One of our favorite producers was David Foster—a man who had launched many people's careers, helped established stars hit new heights, and produced some of the best recordings in pop music history. He had worked with hundreds of stars, including Josh Groban, Michael Bublé, Celine Dion, Whitney Houston, Barbara Streisand, Chicago, Charice, Will.i.am, and many others.

David Foster did very few concerts because he was a pianist and more of a producer than a live performer. Of late, though, he had shown some interest in stepping out of the shadows and had been doing a few live shows. This concert tour had very few stops, and with the closest one to us being the New Jersey suburbs of New York City, we decided to make the four-hour trek.

While my panic-attack situation was getting much better, it was not completely fixed. Being on the sabbatical and off Actos had helped calm me down, but the novelty of traveling to a busy metropolitan area sounded a bit challenging to me. Despite my concern, I really wanted to go to the concert and couldn't let my friend down. This stemmed from a strong desire not to give in to fear.

Following a carefully mapped route, I drove from the Washington suburbs through Baltimore, then eastern Pennsylvania, and eventually into New Jersey. It was a longer route than necessary to avoid the big bridge over the Schuylkill River on Interstate 95 that led toward downtown Philly.

Things went well for the first few hours, despite relentless rain and early evening darkness. As we approached the area of Newark where the concert venue was located, however, suddenly the twelve-lane highway we were on seemed to be leading us straight east into New York City. My heart leapt. My panic returned as the big buildings of Manhattan lurked in the distance. I went a bit crazy worrying about some high bridge that might lie ahead.

As my Impala hurled ever closer to Newark Bay, my pulse skyrocketed. I felt the unknown chemical being released in my stomach. Would I pass out or totally freak out? I tried to bring my emotions under control. Praying silently with all my might, I begged God to help me keep it together. With great relief, I finally saw our desired exit appear on the road signs. It became obvious that we would turn off before the highway headed into New York City. This didn't calm me down instantly, but it gave me hope. Slowly and surely, I turned the steering wheel toward the exit, and we careened around the circular ramp.

At the bottom I slowed considerably and turned toward the stadium. We were out of trouble, at least for the moment. We came to the stadium and quickly found parking. I gave an enormous sigh of relief.

Still, arrival at the stadium held a few anxious moments for me. As I visited this large, unknown structure for the first time, I worried about things like having to ride gigantic escalators that soared to upper decks. This arena did not present such a challenge, however. Once through the turnstiles, we easily found our seats.

Finally we sat down for the concert, and it was magnificent. Peter Cetera was absolutely engaging that night. Ruben Studdard and Katherine Jenkins were also amazing. Hearing the soaring voices and seeing David Foster lead it all made the harrowing trip worth it. Although this kind of situation was what I labeled "difficult fun," it showed me where I stood on my anxiety issue and reaffirmed my need to be on sabbatical.

On the way back to our hotel, I made my friend drive. He didn't want to, but he gave in to the argument that it was only fair since I had driven the five hours to the arena. After a short drive on city streets, it was time to mount the twelve-lane road back out of Newark. He almost pulled the car over when I momentarily objected to his long gaze at the New York skyline. I thought we were going to run off the road and die; he thought I needed to shut up, and he said so. After that I closed my eyes until we were well away from the stadium.

The drive home the next day was uneventful. The trip made me thankful that I had such great friends. As nuts as I could be, they still wanted to be with me.

Making the Most of the Time

Greg and I met in Chicago in the 1980s. He was one of the most interesting people I'd ever known. He was at least six foot two with bright red hair, and his life was mainly about plants. He studied them in college, started a business growing and selling them, and eventually catalogued all the water plant varieties in a seminal book.

He introduced new plants, catalogued previously identified ones, and had strong opinions about them.

I once went on a three-hour walk with Greg through the National Arboretum, laughing all the way. How could anyone make something as boring as plants interesting and funny? But Greg could!

About ten years after graduating from college, Greg married a beautiful lawyer named Sue. I stood up as his best man and had a very enjoyable time doing it. We and his two other groomsmen laughed for an entire weekend as we enjoyed his last days of bachelorhood. We ate and played putt-putt golf and did other such activities.

Greg had grown tens of thousands of wildflowers for his wedding as a special gift to his wife. When we arrived at the church, a florist friend of Greg's was arranging them into huge vases and other arrangements. Unfortunately, a huge hornet buzzed around her when we walked through the flower room for the first time. The next time we walked back through, the hornet had stung her, and one of her hands was wrapped up in a bandage the size of New Mexico. She wept softly as she continued to arrange.

"Hang in there, Delores," Greg said matter of factly, betraying his tough-it-out prescription for life. When we got to another room deeper into the church, the four of us laughed for half an hour at having seen the hornet our first time through and the bandage on our second trip. We also laughed at Greg's lack of compassion. He just wasn't wired for empathy. He didn't really get why we thought it funny, but he laughed with us anyway.

This woman was obviously hurt that Greg hadn't shown concern for her, since she had been doing her work for him. She had the last laugh though. She stopped arranging probably two minutes after we left the room. At the last minute, the thousands of unarranged flowers were hastily carried to the front of the sanctuary. The other groomsmen and I laughed again as we saw the mound of flowers and knew what had happened to the arranger.

Greg had a lot of secrets. The biggest one was that prior to his marriage, he had quite a pornography habit. After his marriage he was physically faithful to his wife (at least as long as I communicated with him). However, he continued the pornography habit. One time his wife called me, distraught because she had found some pornography. She worried that their marriage was a sham. I knew it wasn't. Greg had told me several times how much he loved her, more than anything. I encouraged her to talk to Greg before she did anything rash, and they ended up staying together for many years. I felt thankful that God would use me for good in my friendship with Greg and Sue. We got together every once in a while and our visits were always filled with so much laughter.

While I was on my sabbatical, I decided that I hadn't heard from Greg in too long a time. I looked up the website of his employer to get his current phone number. He had moved from one state to another. I was shocked to learn from the site that he had passed away suddenly.

One website led to another as I frantically tracked down information. Greg had been at a water plant function in Philadelphia. He wasn't feeling well and told everyone he was going back to his room to lie down. A friend became worried about him when he didn't show up for a meeting, so his hotel room was opened. Greg was lying there dead.

I wished I'd contacted Greg much sooner.

Serious Reminders

While I thanked God for the good friends He had given me and for the role many of them played in my healing and growth, I also realized that I had no idea how many years I would have to be a friend to others. Time is so precious to me as a result of many of these losses. Greg was about fifty years old when he passed away. My brother was only forty-six when he died. If I put off phone calls or special occasions or vacations with those I loved, there was no guarantee that I would have time to pursue those things later on. I needed to do whatever God was telling me to do before it was too late.

16

THREE LADIES

MY SABBATICAL WAS ABOUT THE PRESENT, but it was also about the past.

While I thought about some of my scars and how God had healed deep wounds, God also led me to remember some of the people I had admired over the years, and He reminded me of the lessons, good and bad, that I had learned from their lives. By noticing the good in other people, I gained role models for doing life in a rewarding way. There are three ladies that illuminated peace for me, each in their own way. These weren't the only women who brought the gift of peace, but they were each beautiful friends to me in their own ways.

Lena's Peace and Love

As a teenager in college and later as a young adult, no trip back to my hometown in Ohio was complete without a visit to Lena and her husband, Dewey. They were both sweet Christian people with very large personalities. Like many couples that remain together for more than sixty years, they were as different as night and day.

Dewey suffered from significant hearing loss in later years. He had already been a terminally quiet individual who was content to sit and listen for long periods without speaking. This was good, because his wife could talk for hours without taking a breath. When Dewey did have something important to say, he cleared his throat, causing the many folds under his chin to move rhythmically. I used to watch this and imagine it in slow motion. Lena would pause one of her classic stories long enough for "Daddy" to tell me a spiritual insight he had gleaned from his daily devotions. Then Lena resumed her tales of life in the coal-mining camp or of her later life in Cleveland when Dewey had worked at the Dan Dee Pretzel and Potato Chip Company.

Dewey inevitably began his stories with a dramatic statement that made me feel like a bright spotlight was shining right into my heart. After I squirmed for several seconds, Dewey told me some jewel of life that helped me immeasurably in following days. Lena would say as she listened to him, "That's the truth, Daddy." Then Dewey would return to his shell like a turtle frightened by a predator.

As I sat on their sensible green couch with its knitted afghan, I felt incredibly safe. Bombs could fall, tornados could barrel through, but nothing on Earth could hurt me in the middle of all that love.

Lena and Dewey had met at a young age in the coal-mining camp where they had both grown up near Bluefield, West Virginia. Lena loved to tell the story of their marriage. Dewey had persuaded a then fifteen-ish Lena to sneak off to Kentucky, where the marrying age was younger than that of West Virginia. They eventually found someone to do the job, but it was raining horribly that day, so the duly sworn official knelt on the front seat of their car, facing backwards, to perform the ceremony. Lena and Dewey exchanged vows in the back seat of their Buick and then found a motel in which to get better acquainted.

Lena had a thousand stories and seldom repeated any of them other than the marriage tale. She told of coal-mine accidents, floozies who needed running off with big skillets, and tales of premature births. One of her daughters was so small when she was born that Lena and Dewey kept her in a shoe box in the dresser near the radiator. Last I knew their daughter was on the downhill side of seventy, so I guess the Lord helped her make it.

When Dewey grew tired of coal mining, he moved his family to Cleveland, Ohio. Lena made many friends in the northern industrial city and was happy and popular there. She and Dewey stayed strong and trusted in the Lord during their twenty years in the city.

Finally the two of them were too old for city life and wanted to be close to their two daughters, so they moved to a small town near Dayton where my family lived. Lena became disoriented by this second big move. She was angry and unhappy to leave friends in Cleveland.

When Lena moved from Cleveland to my little town, I was in my teens, and she was in her sixties. She was hobbled a bit from having too many big meals and not enough exercise, and she rocked back and forth when she walked. Her personality was fully intact, though, and we became good friends. Lena's smile, laughter, and undivided gaze drew me in. She was present in the moment.

After I moved away for college and came back only for short visits, our time became more precious, Lena's and mine. Maybe I sensed that the end of my peace was coming, since I was beginning to feel jaded in my knowledge of God and would soon go through the questioning time that many young adults face. Our visits followed a familiar pattern. As I came in, she was usually seated in her big chair. I bent over and hugged her. She asked if I wanted anything, and I declined. If she insisted, I asked for a water, and she asked Dewey to get it for me. Or if she was alone, she sent me to the kitchen to "fetch it." Each time I visited, I felt great relief to see her smiling and well.

She spun her stories, and I listened intently. Occasionally I got in a quick-reaction sentence that made her laugh. As we visited, I felt that sense of peace again.

When I was about 20 Dewey was in a terrible car accident and needed to recover for many months on their couch. Finally he was well again and praising Jesus for healing him. He resumed church attendance and was apparently feeling well, but a couple years later, he died quickly, without having been sick at all. Lena lasted a few more years and then joined Dewey in heaven. I didn't return for either of their funerals, though I now wish I had.

Lena taught me a lot about storytelling, comic delivery, peace, and love, but mainly to be present in the moment.

Margaret's Caring Heart

Some years later, after I had moved to Virginia, I met Margaret in one of my church's home Bible studies. Margaret Horton was a proper British ex-patriot who had married an American after World War II. She was strong and stoic and pushing eighty.

Margaret was the center of activity in the Lewinsville, the retirement community in which she lived. She organized Red Hat Society activities and made great efforts to ensure that new residents found a place to fit into her community. Margaret cared about the spiritual and physical welfare of her neighbors, often encouraging people from our church to come over and help them. Margaret even gave up her good wheelchair to a new resident of their community. "You need it more than I do," she told him.

The man just beamed. Margaret had truly given him the Rolls Royce of all wheelchairs. She knew that God would help her make it with her cane. She was right.

One Christmas Margaret Horton persuaded our Bible study group to put on a show for the residents of her community. It was so much fun preparing and performing for the senior citizens. I dressed in my Tigger suit and recited Robert Frost's "Stopping by Woods on a Snowy Evening." One dignified-looking older gentleman in the back recited every word with me. I wouldn't have needed a teleprompter if I had forgotten the words. I wondered if the man appreciated that I did the poem in my best Bullwinkle vocal impersonation. If he minded, he didn't show it. We also did a vignette based on a Chekhov play. It went over quite well with the highly educated clientele of the Lewinsville.

Margaret taught me about serving others, whether or not the help was well received at first. Some people resisted her ideas, but she persevered. Many of her schemes turned out to be great blessings to her community—and to those of us who came to help her.

Margaret Horton's funeral was beautiful as friends and family came to pay their respects. I had to smile when so many Red Hat women filed into the service, dressed in their signature hats and purple outfits. Several testified about how much Margaret had meant to each of them and to the community as a whole.

She taught me and her other friends that service to others changes people. As I thought about Margaret and how she had influenced my life, I realized that I needed to apply her lessons in a fresh way. I had been so caught up in the busyness and press of my job that I had often failed to bless the people at work. God had made me for a purpose, and He wanted me to serve the people He had put into my life, out of love for Him and for them. One life lived for God among others could definitely make a difference.

A Perfect Day

My co-worker and I had just checked into our rooms. The hotel was beautiful. Its palm trees and manicured lawns fed my prior perceptions of Orange County, California. My co-worker, a woman who had been a friend for many years, and I had flown into LAX from Washington DC the evening before for a work-related con-ference—a gathering of business and scientific personnel from university and non-profit research institutions as well as federal government types like us. But before the conference began that evening, we planned to spend the day at Disneyland; it would be my first-ever visit to the Magic Kingdom on the West Coast. The conference could not have been further from our minds as we opened Disneyland that morning.

Although I had tried to keep it a secret, I'd had a major work crush on this woman for many years. She was a great friend, and we had worked together for more than ten years. Her beautiful blonde hair and twinkling eyes made me a little bit high each time I saw her. How amazing it was to have worked in the same office with someone like this for so long. I wasn't the only person who thought this way about my friend. Everyone (almost) liked her.

Now we were to spend an entire day at the happiest place on Earth. Neither of us were married, although she was in a serious relationship. We were friends of the highest magnitude and, as far as I could tell, we each enjoyed the other's company.

A few raindrops didn't deter us as we parked the rental car and headed for the entrance. January was not a busy time at the park, and we had no trouble gaining admission and walking to the rides. The rain picked up, and we decided to get blue rain ponchos and check out Mickey Mouse's house. After the brief tour, we were ushered into the photo room to pose with Mickey. We laughed as we waited. Eventually Mickey embraced us, and someone took our picture. I always thought that Mickey saw in our eyes how much we loved him, because he said a special goodbye to us and paused a moment longer than necessary when he shook my hand.

Every experience that day was magical. We laughed our way from the Haunted Mansion to It's a Small World. After the ride we got hot chocolate and took cover from the rain under a tent. Suddenly

I looked in her eyes, and I saw so much pure love. Not a sexual or possessive love but a God-given love of one earth traveler to another. Her rain poncho was pulled back to reveal a bit of her golden locks and tastefully adorned ears. I snapped a quick photograph of the moment—I wanted to hold onto the day forever. What was I doing at Disneyland with a woman like this? I wondered.

We rode the flume at Splash Mountain and took in *The Lion King* show. Each experience was more fun than the last. Finally it was time to begin exiting the park in deference to their winter hours and our conference reception scheduled for later that evening. We looked through the gift shop on our way out. I couldn't resist buying her a pair of Mickey Mouse earrings. She took off the earrings she was wearing and put on the Mickeys right then. I loved seeing the smile on her face that day. It was truly a perfect rainy day.

I had felt so much peace with this woman at Disneyland. On the plane ride home, I still felt calm with her. When we returned to work and our boss became hyper and started yelling, everything was okay, because she was around. Every once in a while, she wore the Mickey earrings to work, and I remembered our fun day. I felt so much peace—it made me believe that life was going to be okay.

Treasuring People

The rain on the roof of my sunroom reminded me of that perfect day. While God had allowed harmful events in my life that had scarred me in the short run but had healed into something beautiful for Him, He had also given me wonderful memories that in some ways meant more to me than my scars. Such memories had fed my soul for years. I looked back on these days and saw them as the dessert at the banquet of my life. I thanked God for the lessons I had learned in my past from Lena and Margaret, and my co-worker. God knows that I prayed for more perfect days in my future like the one I'd had at Disneyland.

17

RESURRECTING DREAMS

THE START OF A NEW WEEK brought the beginning of a new book. Jentezen Franklin's *Believe That You Can* was literally another godsend. This book was all about living one's dreams.

At this point in my life, I felt far from inspired. Many of my dreams (I'd always wanted to write a book, and I'd also hoped to act in a movie one day) seemed dead and buried. But as I read Franklin's book, I allowed myself to believe that a new future was possible for me, and my dreams began to reawaken.

One of the most inspiring concepts for me in Franklin's book had to do with the resurrection of dreams. Franklin explained that God often gives His children dreams of great accomplishments for

His glory. These dreams are linked to the great harvest that God desires to take place in the earth; in this harvest of souls, thousands will come to Jesus for salvation. But so often we let our dreams die over time. God watches this happen and uses this season of death to help us sort through our motives. When we are sure our dreams are dead, God speaks a word of life to those dreams. He resurrects them, first in our minds and then by stirring our faith. We begin to believe that maybe, just maybe, our dreams might not be so farfetched after all. Maybe, if we link our dreams to God's purposes, we can see them come true.

This second book by Franklin further changed my life by helping me see that the stagnation of the past several years was not the end of my dreams. God had more for me to do. If I listened to His voice and followed His lead, I would see many dreams come true and miracles done.

Room for Creativity

I knew the primary reason I had been created: to know and worship God. But when it came to living out God's dreams for me, I wondered if He expected me to be or do anything in particular. How would I know the specifics of His purpose for my life? I found my answer in the Bible.

In the parable of the talents, God expected the servants to do something with the money, or talents, He had given them. But here is what I found: God wasn't specific about how the people were to invest His money. He simply made it clear that He didn't expect them to bury their talents in the backyard and then give them back to God at the end of their lives.

At the beginning of the Bible, God told Adam and Eve to take care of the garden of Eden. He didn't get specific with them either by requesting that they build topiaries or come up with creative landscaping ideas, but it was clear that He intended them to work and take care of the garden.

God wanted me to accomplish things for Him, but as I studied and prayed, I came to see that He had left me some room for creativity. He had given me parameters (like being honest, putting Him first, loving others), but He had also given me room to be creative in how I delighted Him and others. I didn't need to be afraid of missing His plan; I just needed to stay in contact with Him every day and accept His gentle course corrections and advice as I moved forward in service to Him. Along the way I would have great potential to help others and teach them about God through my experiences.

One of my role models in this was my pastor and teacher, Steve Reynolds. He had found a big part of his ministry in a creative way: he had founded his weight-loss ministry, Losing to Live, after he had lost over a hundred pounds. His love for people also motivated him to write his book, *Bod 4 God*, in order to help other people in need. Pastor Steve took Christianity to a practical level, and that made an impression on me. Using his talents to do something of practical good gave weight to the gospel, no pun intended.

Dreaming a Little

One of my earliest recollections was my desire to be creative. From the time I was small, I had never wanted to do the same old thing but had always wanted to create new things. Entertaining people was one of my passions, though it had never fit well with my life as a government division director. I thought back to some of the highlights of my show-biz career.

When I was five, I wrote my first song: "Way Back When the Pumpkin Skin Was Very, Very Ripe." This was performed live for my mother and father to the accompaniment of my drum solo on the bottom of a small metal trashcan.

Three years later I found my brother's old joke book and memorized jokes. I enjoyed telling many of these gems to my school friends and also to my parents.

When I was twelve, my buddy, Phil Suttles, and I entertained our entire sixth-grade class with an uproarious (we thought) magic act and a health-elixir commercial. The magic act bombed, but the commercial got big laughs. The elixir, when ingested orally, gave the recipient (me) an incredible ability to perform ordinary tasks four or five times faster than normal. Phil provided the elixir and manned the stereo. The "before" scene showed me sweeping the floor with a 45-rpm record played at 33 1/3 rpm in the background. The music was slow, and I moved slowly. For the "after," Phil turned the music up to 98 rpm. I hurled myself around the stage, knocking things over and greatly entertaining my still unseasoned elementary school peers.

I found that day that there was nothing as amazing as hearing one hundred children laughing uncontrollably over my humor. Show biz: I was hooked. It was all the attention I craved and absolutely what I was born to do.

In junior high Phil and I were reunited in an effort to publish a local version of *Mad Magazine.* Unfortunately our partnership ended over creative differences and awkward junior-high issues.

In high school I joined the choir. I was just fine being one of seventy-five people up on stage. We got to wear sophisticated dark-blue robes, and our director was extremely good. We learned all kinds of music and grew as musicians. The choir also put on a big musical each year; I participated in *The King and I* and *Fiddler on the Roof.* I even had a supporting actor role in *Fiddler* as Lazar Wolf

Also in high school I was voted best student director for my seminal work on Thornton Wilder's *Our Town.* Okay, this really wasn't a big deal, but I had fun and further got hooked on entertainment.

My memories were mostly fun, but they stirred creative desire in my heart. What might God have in store for me in months to come? After retirement? Little did I know that He would have a special role for me to play in serving Him even before my sabbatical came to an end.

Planning for Service

Living out God's purpose for my life, I also realized, included not only creativity but planning. At times God wanted His people to take huge steps of faith without knowing where they were going, but I noticed that God seemed happy with me when I planned ahead in my service for Him—as long as I invited Him into my planning process. A lot of people, I had noticed, didn't accomplish very much in life because they didn't understand this principle. Life passed them by, and they voiced regrets about how little they'd done over the years.

One year I served as the Angel Tree chair for my local church, planning and executing a drive that included buying forty gifts for the children of inmates. One young family in the church took a single child's name, but at the last minute they called and said that they couldn't possibly buy and wrap a gift (a small child's toy) because they were so busy. I scratched my head and laughed to myself. At the time I was working full time and in graduate school and serving in several other ministries at church, but these two full-grown adults hadn't been able to fit it into their busy schedules to buy one toy and wrap it in three weeks' time. The funny part is that, being Christmastime, I knew they would be shopping and wrapping many toys for their own children. Still, this one task had overwhelmed them—because they didn't understand the impor-tance of planning.

On the other hand, some people accomplished a lot.

My mother was one of these people. At almost ninety she still planned and executed dinners for thirty, forty, or more at church. She also visited sick people and shut-ins from her congregation. She even served as an emergency babysitter once in a while for the kindergarten-to-second-grade set. All her life she had been a hard worker—and a great planner.

One of my mom's favorite sayings was "Write it down!" Her friends kidded her about her thorough note-taking at various church meetings. I was proud of my mom for who she was and for all the people she'd helped over the years. Just a few of her accomplishments that required planning included leadership roles with WWII WAVES, Girl Scouts, Cub Scouts, Friendship Force International, Alpha Course, Dinners for Eight, and the United Methodist Women She had also been a missions supporter, even taking trips all over the globe to verify mission results. She had been a Bible study leader and had taught fourth-grade Sunday school for twenty years.

For her effort my mom was rewarded with a lifetime of amazing experiences and a wonderful relationship with God. She met Mother Theresa, rode a camel and an elephant, flew on tiny mission planes in Africa, got teargassed in Korea, walked in the holy lands where Jesus walked, met teachers and evangelists who went on to national prominence, loved thousands of people in practical ways, and received love in return from countless relatives, friends, and perfect strangers.

In the parable of the talents, Jesus tried to explain His disdain for people playing it safe to the extent of doing nothing. We were all given minds, resources (large or small), other people, books, the Internet, and an environment in which to work. God expected us to take the talents or gifts we possessed and turned those into something for Him.

God didn't necessarily want me to become a preacher or a missionary to a far-off country. Our heavenly Father wanted me to take a part in caring for His world and the people He created to fill it. If my role was to be a friend to one neighbor, God wanted me to show all the love I could muster to that individual. God's plan was that I enjoy working for His glory. That might include a government job that would pay the bills and give me a chance to care for my co-workers. It might include hobbies that would lead me to bless children or encourage others who were trying to lose weight. There was so much to be done in the world and so many opportunities for me to help others.

If I prayerfully planned, God would use me to do more than if I failed to plan. Some things could only be done with years of planning and step-by-step progress toward the final stage of the plan. If I got busy and served God intentionally with the gifts and talents He had given me, I imagined that I just might hear Jesus say, "Come unto me, all ye that labour and are heavy laden, and I will give you rest" (Matt. 11:28).

The Meaning of Life

As I listened every day to God's voice in my daily devotions and through many good books, I began to find new meaning in life. I wasn't put on Earth to live a short life and die a meaningless death. God had breathed His life into my lungs and brought me to this place of sabbatical in order to continue perfecting me so that I could better serve Him and others.

God had a plan for my life, and He eagerly wanted to share that plan with me. No previous sin or problem could prevent my dreams from coming true if I dedicated my dreams to God and trusted Him for their outcome.

Why was I here on this earth? This was one of the big questions of my sabbatical, but I wasn't looking for an abstract answer. I wanted to know who God wanted me to be for the rest of my life. Not just what I should *do* but who I was to *be* at my core. How did He want to inform who I was with His Word? What was the path He wanted me to walk for His glory?

My sabbatical was a spiritual journey as much as a physical one. Taking time off and decompressing for a while began to change who I was as I opened myself up to the God of the universe and His Son, Jesus. God had been waiting to gather me into His arms, to take me on His lap and tell me secrets about my life. As I drew near to Him, He relieved me of my addictions and the diseases that had hindered me and showed me His beautiful plan of freedom and purpose for my life.

18

Enjoying the Present

In December, two months into my sabbatical, the world outside intruded—I was called for a job interview with the Army. I wasn't ready to go back to work yet, even though I was feeling over the panic attacks, but the government sometimes took months to clear a person to enter on duty (and start drawing a salary again), so I needed to give some attention to future plans.

My decision to go on the interview was a difficult one. Having been a Navy civilian employee for more than twenty years, it was hard for me to think about working for the Army. While I felt the novelty of considering something new, I knew too much about the Army to be excited about working for them in my specialty of contract policy. But I was burning through my retirement money, and the funds wouldn't last forever. I didn't want to regret not finding out more about this job opportunity, so I decided to put on a suit, pretend I was ready and go.

As I walked into the security hut outside the heavily guarded building, I realized that my fantasy sabbatical world was not the real world. The machine guns gently cradled in the arms of the camouflage-clad guards were off-putting. I quickly signed the admittance roster and provided interviewer's name. A nice soldier ushered me outside into the cold to wait for my escort. The escort took several minutes to make his way from the distant office to the checkpoint where visitors arrive. It gave me time to study the tank parked in the front yard of the facility. It was big and intimidating, while I felt small and not ready to work for these people. The escort finally arrived, and we moved away from the machine guns and in the direction from which he'd come.

Our hard shoes clicked heavily on the asbestos-tiled floors. I fought the urge to tap dance. As we walked, I pumped my guide for information about the office and the person interviewing me. By the time we reached the suite of executive offices, I knew a lot more than I had before about the culture, the boss, and the food options (there weren't any). I liked to think that the escort was rooting for me in the interview, but maybe that was just my imagination.

The stoic woman now before me grilled me for the better part of forty-five minutes. She seemed very interested in my sabbatical and perhaps a bit worried that I was a nut case. Although I was somewhat relieved that I probably wouldn't be getting a job offer, since the interview made clear that I was overqualified for this job, reality did set in about my reentry to the workforce. Federal managers would likely be very suspicious about why a twenty-some-year government worker would suddenly quit outright and then try to come back. Feds in their right mind didn't quit six years before retirement eligibility. At least healthy ones didn't.

As the interview concluded, my Army questioner shook my hand and said with great compassion, "Take care of yourself. Really." I think she meant it—in a genuine you-are-sort-of-scaring-me way.

As I clicked my way back down the long hallways, I didn't say much more to my escort. I didn't worry so much about what I would eventually do for a job as I did over the thought that I might never want to go back to the government.

Career and Retirement in View

In the wake of the job interview, I began to think more specifically about my immediate future as well as my long-term future. Jentezen Franklin's book *Believe That You Can* had stirred me to pursue God's dreams for my life, and my growing understanding of wise financial planning motivated me to consider my practical needs. In many ways my sabbatical was crystallizing my understanding of what God wanted to do with my life.

I thought about my prior career in the Navy and also with the government agency where I'd most recently worked. Being a federal division director had allowed me to learn and grow as a person. I'd helped many people and been helped by so many great folks. I also felt a sense of accomplishment for my small part in the gigantic missions of the organizations I'd served. I realized that I wanted to go back to this kind of work, if I could.

From a financial angle as well it became clear to me that I really ought to return to the government and finish my federal career. Just six years from retirement, I realized that it would be irresponsible of me to walk away from all I'd built, as I had no other immediate option to ensure the same level of financial stability for my future. Going back to the government wouldn't make me rich in retirement, but it would allow me to live inexpensively and relatively well.

So I made a call to my former boss. He was surprised to hear from me so soon after I had quit, but he seemed glad to get the call. I explained to him that I wanted to discuss the possibilities of returning to my old agency, possibly in February (I had a trip planned for early January). He was interested in discussing it further and made it clear that the agency could find somewhere for me to work. He would need to speak with his boss to confirm exactly where they could use me.

A couple hours later my former boss and his boss called me back: I had a job with the agency if I wanted it! This was a tremendous relief. At least I wouldn't have to worry about finding another job or, worse yet, *not* finding another job.

With my financial needs secured until I retired, my mind began to race about the possibilities for my future beyond retirement. I would definitely not be ready to permanently exit the workforce at that point in my life, age 56. In fact, I wasn't sure that God ever planned for any of us to completely quit working. Even if I took a pay cut or worked without pay, work makes me happy.

While I hoped to keep getting paid beyond federal retirement, I hoped whatever I did would be something more creative and fun than government service. I wanted to develop my other talents, interests, and ambitions.

My sabbatical musings led me back to the creative urges I'd had since childhood. So much of my enjoyment in the last fifteen to twenty years had involved attending shows of all kinds. I'd gone ape over small programs at local theaters, large concerts in stadiums, smaller concerts at a favorite outdoor amphitheater, and movies. Over the course of my time off, I began to realize that I would be very happy working in theater or entertainment someday.

As I prayed into these desires, I didn't have an immediate answer as to how they would eventually flesh out. My mind, however, was totally energized by the possibilities. Should I try to resurrect my acting skills from long ago? Was I supposed to be a writer and stay behind the scenes? Should I become a concert promoter who brought entertainment to waiting fans? All these ideas released a great deal of energy within me.

But what did God have in mind? While I was free to be creative and responsible to plan, I didn't want to blindly follow my own plans and ideas. I wanted to be in the flow of what God was doing in the world, in our country, and in my community. I would let these ideas percolate until after my upcoming Christmas trip to Ohio and my New Year's trip to Disney World.

Creating A Christmas Memory

As Christmas approached, my sabbatical was fully engaged. At this point I turned my focus from quiet time alone and thoughts about my future to the holiday season. On the day before I was supposed to travel home to Ohio for the holidays, I went to see Handel's Messiah at the Kennedy Center with a friend. I was excited to take a break from study and prayer to get out and about in downtown Washington.

Our first stop was for a pricey dinner at the Octagon Room, located near the White House. The food was exquisite and the artwork legendary. The sights and smells were the closest thing to Mom's house at Christmas, but with an uptown flair.

After the gourmet meal we headed for Concert Hall, one of three theaters inside the Kennedy Center. The stately building always looked beautiful at night. Since I knew my way around the area, it was easy to find our way into the parking structure. Emerging into the Kennedy Center from its parking garage below was a familiar pleasure. It felt as if we were secret agents sneaking into the Kremlin. We bought a souvenir and a few Christmas gifts at the gift shops and headed for our seats.

The evening was wonderful. The hall was grand and glorious without being over the top. Lightly and tastefully adorned for Christmas, Concert Hall had never looked better. Red banners and evergreen boughs warmed the spirit. One of my former friends from work sang in the choir each year. It was fun to see his bearded mug in the choir howling out the big bass parts I'd sung this work in high school. All the scriptures associated with the Messiah brought home to me the message of the season, Jesus was born.

After the wonderful dinner and concert, we went to my car for the drive home. Since we had parked under the building, we were surprised, as we drove out into the night, to be greeted by rapidly falling snow. It was a couple inches deep on the streets and looked even thicker in the grass. We elected to go home through Rock Creek Park, a two-thousand-acre urban park in DC's northwest quadrant. It was a magical scene on an ordinary day, but with this beautiful snowfall, it was overwhelmingly magnificent. After dropping off my friend, I found my way home. I headed to the sunroom and sat in my La-Z-Boy as the snow came down quietly in the glowing moonlight outside. God was alive in everything I saw and perceived. So much gratitude flooded my body, mind, and soul. I began to praise and worship the King. How had this old sinner gotten so blessed at this point in his life?

Family Christmas

The road to Ohio from Washington traversed the sometimes beautiful mountains of West Virginia. After ninety minutes of rather flat terrain with a few hills from my home in the Washington area, the mountains began abruptly just past Hancock, Maryland. The Christmas trip was usually a beautiful one with snow on a few mountaintops but little trouble with the road conditions.

This year I began the trip thinking that the roads were clear; I made good time through the mountains and past Wheeling, West Virginia. Without much warning, however, the weather turned nasty only a few minutes into Ohio. Before long my car and thousands of others were creeping along at twenty miles an hour. Several months earlier such a sudden change may have brought on substantial worry and even some physical symptoms, but for some reason I remained calm. The scene was quite beautiful and the tail light were half the traditional colors of Christmas.

After inching along for more than two hours, the traffic came to a halt. I decided to get out of my car and grab a snack from the trunk. It was then that I realized that the road was covered with approximately two inches of ice. Miraculously the traffic started moving again. We crawled up a long incline to find two semis jack-knifed at the top of a small hill. Fortunately a wrecker had towed one of the semis off the road, allowing us a lane to get by.

Safely at my mother's home that night, I thought back over the trip and how far God had brought me. Instead of having panic attacks, I had kept my mind on God's power to keep me through a curveball that life had thrown. In my heart I had known that I would make it home and have a storybook Christmas with my mom and other family members. Perhaps I was learning another level of the meaning of faith.

A few days later our extended family crammed into Mom's small living room. The scene of so many wonderful family moments from my childhood was alive once more with my mom's great grandchildren crawling around or toddling into the playroom. Every inch of my mom's house was dedicated to God and to family. The paint-by-number Lord's Supper that my sister had done when she was in high school hung over the breakfast table. My vacation Bible school Jesus picture smiled back at Mom in her bedroom. The guestroom had pictures of myself and the rest of the family posing with Scooby Doo or Mickey Mouse or some other life-sized character at one of the many theme parks we'd visited together. And the big bookcase in the living room had all of the grandchildren pictures carefully arranged by age.

As everyone tore into their carefully wrapped gifts, squeals of laughter emanated from the kids of all ages. My collection of ties and business shirts was augmented with cute homemade gifts from some of the younger set. My place, as always, was next to Mom, holding a large trash bag. The relatives tried to make baskets from every corner of the living room with their wadded-up gift wrap.

This caused me look everyone in the face several times during the evening, even if I occasionally took one of the missiles to the face.

This Christmas was one of the best we'd had as a family, for one reason in particular. Mom's years were growing short. This turned out to be her second to last Christmas with us. Each of us knew that she was the glue that held the family together. These holidays together were ten times more precious just because we all knew that time was running out.

After the voices died down and the last grandchild had hugged and kissed her way to the door, Mom and I rounded up the scattered dishes. I savored the silence and the moments with her as I'd never done quite so completely. As I washed and she dried, a single tear slid down my face.

19

DISCOVERY

THE BIG THEME OF MY SABBATICAL, as I saw it, was learning to shed my fear so that I could live in peace and thus live out God's purpose for my life. God had made me to be something special; He had formed all the intricate quirks of my personality and the likes and dislikes that caused me to be unique. He did not intend me to spend my time worrying about my life ending. I had been created for love and for eternity. My job was to be creative in becoming the real me—the person He made me to be in service to Himself and to others.

To know the real me, I needed to know the only real One in the universe: God. My life was not about me but about Him. All the misguided "me first" dialogue of our culture was fool's gold. I knew I could never make myself happy abandoning others and seeking selfish goals. It was in abandoning self and seeking after God that I would truly find the real person I was meant to be.

Finding the true me had been a process long in the making. My initial commitment to Christ was just the first step in a relationship that will last to infinity. Like many Christians, I had false expectations that commitment to Christ should have led me to instant perfection. At least for me, that hasn't been my experience.

Finding Myself through Grace and Growth

In 1982, not many months past college graduation, I moved to Chicago for my first major job. Throughout my years in there, I felt estranged from God. There were a lot of reasons and partially this was just the process of me shedding my Mom's faith and developing my own. As a result of deep questions about myself and about God's character, I began to doubt God's loving nature. My church experiences up to this point had made me wonder if God really loved me as I was or if He was a judge eager to see me fail. Like the prodigal son, I determined that my way was the more reasonable option. Considerable riotous living ensued.

I've heard it said that our choice is not between God and the devil but between God and ourselves. For a few years, I served myself. I led the life of a depressed clown. On the outside, I tried to make my life appear as one big party. This inspired a lot of envy around the office as I told about one bash after another. On the inside, however, I was very much alone. Relationships didn't work for me, because I didn't like myself, and I knew that the way I was living was wrong. It came down to this thought: *if I'm giving up heaven for you, why won't you even do the dishes?*

After years of trying to do things my way, I was ready to come back home. By this time I lived in the DC area (God had answered my prayer to live in Washington despite my rebellion!), and I had been with the Navy for several years. As I stood at the sink in my apartment doing dishes, God sang to me. It sounded like a Father calling His son home. It sounded as if He missed me. Boy, did I miss Him. He'd kept me from dying at least a couple times, I was sure of that. I'd taken some awful chances late at night in downtown Chicago. God's sweet voice was more than I could resist. I headed back to church and back to the Lord.

Although I had decided to return to God, I wasn't excited about coming back to church people at first. I was suspicious of their supposed piety and the judgmental attitudes I'd experienced in earlier church experiences. But our wise Father had a plan for me.

I also had a plan. I would look up four churches in the phone book and go to each one on successive Sundays starting on New Year's Day. After the fourth one, I'd decide which of them was the least offensive and attend there. My hopes were not high.

On New Year's Eve I went out with some people I barely knew from my apartment building. They didn't want me staying at home for the holiday, and bringing me with them also helped add to the size of their posse, which they probably felt increased their fun quotient. While I didn't drink a lot or party hard, since I had recently returned to the fold, the New Year's partying lasted until the early morning of the first. We even had a pizza at two thirty in the morning. When the alarm rang on Sunday morning, January 1, I decided to sleep in and begin my church-hunting scheme on week two.

The following Sunday I went to the second church on my list. The pastor, Wendell Cover, was a sweet man with a real talent for preaching practical messages. His church, Word of Life, was not exactly my brand, but about thirty minutes into the service, during a time of fellowship when everyone walked around and shook everyone else's hands, many men and women welcomed me. These people made me feel as if there was room for me at Word of Life Church, and I took it as God's signal to look no further.

When Pastor Cover began to preach about God's love, I started to cry. After a while I didn't bother trying to hide my tears. At the end of the message, I came forward to the altar to make my rededication to God official. I was God's little boy again—at age twenty-nine.

Unlike the stories in some Christian books and movies, I didn't immediately begin living happily ever after. A lot of wreckage from my past needed to be cleaned up. Most of my twenties had been lost to me because of depression and sadness over many things. Each week I came to church, and many times I cried.

But I found out that God could heal depression in a word when I went to a Christian conference in California with friends. During one of the sessions, the attendees were given an opportunity to be prayed for one on one. The man who prayed for me asked me some questions, and I explained that I battled depression. Then he said something that he had definitely received straight from the throne of God: "Tell David that he doesn't have to die, because he is already dead. He died with my Son in baptism and rose again. Now he is alive forever."

This prayer changed my life, and it remained with me after that day. Over the years it helped me battle any attempt by depression to get another foothold in my life. I knew that this man's statement was from God because, first, it lined up with God's Word, the Bible, and second, it continued to bring life whenever I repeated it. Those first few months, as God healed my hurts and answered my questions, my heart gradually softened.

Finding the Faithful Father

In time I figured out that Word of Life had an active homeless ministry. The church members took buses into Washington DC on Sunday mornings and picked up the homeless. They brought men and women to church for the service and then served them a good breakfast. The homeless, mainly men, stunk, and some were high on alcohol or drugs. But God showed me His love for these people who could be trophies of His grace, and I felt a natural bond with them because I had also strayed from God's plan for my life. Of course, I'd had the good taste to do it while living uptown—or so my pride tried to tell me.

Working in the kitchen and helping prepare breakfasts for the homeless, I met some great Christians, including Lane Helvie. Lane invited me to become his roommate, which allowed me to save for my first house. He taught me something about Christian service and about maintaining a healthy perspective through times of transition. He eventually met his wife to be, and I moved.

Even with good role models like Lane, I was still having trouble trusting God, partly because of fellow Christians who didn't model Christ very well to me, a recently restored believer. As I tried to help around church at one activity or another, I often heard Christians gossiping, judging, or otherwise not acting in a very Christian manner. This confused me. It almost made me revert to my prior view of God as an angry, judging Father. Jesus was fine with me, but I didn't want to hear about the heavenly Father.

God knew how to fix my misperceptions. As I worshiped one day at Word of Life, God showed me a vision. In the vision I was a lamb, and I wandered off from the flock and got dirty. I was embarrassed about how muddy and dirty I was. Suddenly a smiling Super Jesus flew over me in the sky. He swooped down and stood near me, and He spoke in loving tones. I shivered with cold in the mud.

Jesus reached down and picked me up. I worried at first that He might get mud on Himself, but to my surprise, the more He petted my wooly coat, the whiter my wool became. Soon I was a shiny Clorox white!

Jesus then carried me into a huge ornate castle. Tall doors opened, and Jesus carried me to the Father and laid me right in the Father's lap. They laughed together about my wide-eyed expression and my loving nature. I had been so afraid of the Father, but Jesus showed me that His Father was a loving being. The two of them together had great joy, and they hugged me a lot. It was like the best family anyone ever enjoyed.

For almost a year, I saw this vision over and over in various forms, with subtle changes or additions. God drilled its lessons deep into my heart: The Father loved me and was joyful about receiving me to Himself, because Jesus had taken care of my whitening.

I wondered if the vision would continue throughout my lifetime, but Jesus eventually brought it to a conclusion. While I worshiped in a service one day, He showed me a picture of Himself as Super Jesus and me as a lamb. As I watched, I turned into a boy of ten or twelve years old, and Jesus took my hand and walked away with me. I realized that my time of relating to God as just a lamb was ending; I was growing up. But Jesus would stay with me and help me grow to full maturity. I was happy as I watched Jesus and the young boy walk away. I would kind of miss the lamb though.

It's All about God

God reaffirmed His love to me at a Christian conference soon after I'd returned to Him. I'd gone to a conference in San Antonio, Texas, to help reestablish my close relationship with Him. It had more great classes, large-group sessions, and worship times than I could have imagined. The week was packed with helpful information and meaningful spiritual experiences.

My heart was now tender toward the Lord, but I also slowly became overwhelmed with the depths to which I'd sunk in my rebellious years. On the fourth day of the five-day conference, I wanted to hide because of my sin and my emotional tiredness. Instead of sitting that morning with the few friends I'd met at the conference, I sat in the back row of the large chapel. As worship choruses were led up front, I sat in the back hoping that no one, not even God, would see me.

All of a sudden, I heard laughing. It was gentle at first, but it grew louder. I was almost embarrassed for whoever was laughing so much during the worship time. In my spirit I asked, "What's so funny?"

"I'm laughing because you're trying to hide from Me in a church," the voice said. Instantly I knew that it was God the Father. Obviously there was nothing I could say in return.

It was a significant moment in my thought life. I'd never heard God laugh before. In my mind God was a lightning-bolt-throwing, angry-looking dictator from above. I had never understood this happy side of Him in years past. But it made sense. If God had made us in His image and we laugh, why wouldn't He laugh sometimes too?

That worship service changed my relationship with God in a short amount of time. It gave me a more balanced view of our Father. He might get angry sometimes, but He also took great delight in His children. God was a smiling God.

While I wasn't made to live in the past, being on sabbatical gave me a good chance to reflect on my past and recognize the decisions that had led me into trouble and the ones that had led me to godly success. Had that relationship brought me closer to God or taken me further away? Had my choice to attend party after party moved me forward spiritually or backward? Who was I? Who did I want to be?

As I sat in my sunroom thinking about who I had been and who the real me was, I became reacquainted with a truth I already knew: the real me was all about God, not about me at all.

20

JANUARY JOYS

THE FIRST ADVENTURE OF MY SABBATICAL, the short one to New York City (in which I had freaked out at a Broadway show), hadn't turned out too well (comically badly, really). My third adventure, a longer trip to Florida over New Year's, was everything I wanted and more. Well past my initial period of decompression, it was time for my sabbatical to include some risk taking and novelty seeking. I had meant the time off to be about active resting, not going into a coma.

By January my medication change had all but eliminated my anxiety problem. While the diabetes drug Actos had been extremely effective in lowering my blood sugar, it seemed more and more certain that it been one of the root causes of my anxiety problem. Now, more than six weeks away from it, I felt like a new turtle. There were no feelings of pseudo heart attacks or extreme fear. I was much happier in general. Of course, being off work, resting a lot, and growing spiritually through prayer, Bible study, and reading other books contributed to my increasing calm as well. By now I was ready for some fun and adventure.

Orlando or Bust

I had made plans to spend a week in Orlando in early January. I would enjoy the first few days with friends, and then I would connect with family members to attend the Walt Disney World Marathon Weekend. My niece, Sarah, would be running in the race with a friend of hers. I loved Disney World, and I loved my niece and her daughter, Kinsley, and the rest of my family—the combination was wonderful. The whole group was a party and my expectations were high.

I had decided to take Amtrak for the trip. Riding in a reserved sleeper car compartment from Washington to Orlando for eighteen hours, I thought, would be an adventure. Though the little compartment was cramped, it was private, and I could watch movies on my portable DVD player. The train pulled out of Union Station, and we were off, riding the rails.

Meals were served in the dining car. Those traveling alone, as I was, were seated at tables with other passengers, who quickly became new acquaintances. The food was pretty good too. I met another writer and his wife. We exchanged pleasantries over delicious pasta dishes and became fast friends. Although not well known, this new writing friend still gave me hope that getting published could happen. The rhythmic clacking of train on the tracks gave the whole evening a dramatic tone.

When it was time to sleep, the seat in my compartment became a bed. I couldn't quite stretch out completely, but almost. I quickly fell asleep with the rhythmic swaying of the train. It crossed my mind that the train could wreck and I would be hurled thousands of feet into some tangerine orchard in Northern Florida, but I decided not to worry about something for a change. For some reason I was able to put fear quickly out of my mind. I woke up at some of the overnight station stops, but each time, the train was soon rolling again, and I was no doubt snoring again.

As dawn broke, I woke up and put my seat back up. The dawn was beautiful, and the Florida countryside offered an ever-changing view. Due to unusually cold temperatures, farmers were out in their fields trying to save their crops. While I had empathy for them, I was fascinated with all their activity and smoke pots.

When I arrived in Orlando, I had a short drive in the rental car to collect a friend at the airport. I enjoyed my few days with friends and then headed to Disney World to meet up with my niece and her family.

Theme parks had always provided me a great diversion from my cares, and this particular trip had come at a terrific time as well. I had relaxed and de-stressed for three months; now I could really have fun and enjoy people and external stimuli. The whole trip was an adventure—the train, the friend time and the family time.

The marathon was amazing. I watched and cheered as my niece and her running buddy raced through the various kingdoms of Walt Disney World. Sometimes I was by myself and other times I'd hang out with my other relatives. I used my Park Hopper Option to get into the various parks so I could wave to her as she barreled through Epcot Center, the Animal Kingdom, and the Magic Kingdom. I found a place and waited for Sarah and her friend to come jogging by. They reacted happily to my shouts of encouragement. The two ladies courageously kept the faith and kept going. After a mere seven hours and change, they stumbled across the finish line victorious—meaning that they completed the marathon before it ended and they didn't need to be hospitalized. I was extremely proud of my niece for completing the race. She set a goal, trained hard and completed the course.

I had never had a bucket list before my sabbatical, but during my time away from work, the adventures I had helped me imagine and dream about adventures yet to come—particularly as my anxiety diminished daily. I ended my sabbatical with a bucket list.

High in the Spirit

One typical Saturday night not long after my trip, I decided to attend a new-to-me worship service. I was growing tired of going out socially, even for dinner. I'd planned social time too well for the sabbatical. As it wore on, the times with God became sweeter and more precious than my favorite past time—eating out. I felt compelled to attend this service near my house that friends had told me about. I was eager to see if the good things I'd heard were true. Several friends regularly attended and one of them had invited me. The sabbatical gave me enough time to remember their kind invitation and arrange to attend. During the rat race days, I never seemed to have a Saturday night free—or if I did, I was too tired to go out.

As I found my way to the basement of the church, I was always fond of this neighborhood in Washington DC just over the border from Maryland. Lights lit the trees around the building and a few people milled around outside the Church. My sabbatical was well in progress, and I was loving my relaxed times with the Lord.

All the cars were parked behind the church, so I assumed that the back door was the way into the lower level of the church. I headed down the stairs to a lighted area and found the basement alive with people talking and musicians warming up. I searched the room for the familiar faces of those who had invited me. I was amazed at the bright smiles and lighthearted atmosphere given off by those about to worship. Children ran around the nearly indestructible basement, their laughter filling the place up. The happiness and joy were contagious. I felt the love.

A friend saw me from across the room and headed my way. He greeted me with a hug, and we caught up for few minutes while we waited for the worship to start. He had previously done a sabbatical of a couple years, thanks to some hefty savings and several roommates to share expenses. I had lunched with him earlier in my own sabbatical and learned a lot from him. Now he had invited me to lose myself in worship and focus on Jesus.

I'd experienced many types of church services over the years, from the highly structured Catholic mass to extremely loose house-church formats. This Saturday night service focused on praise and worship. For an hour and often longer, it would be all about freestyle worship. I liked this, because I could lose myself in praising Jesus without being concerned that it would end before I got my praise on. The lead singer was a woman I'd heard sing before. Her voice was soothing, and she played a mean piano. They sang a lot of familiar songs from other church I'd attended, but also a few new ones.

As the service started, I raised my hands and began singing. Before long I was lost in the joy of the Lord. All cares melted away as I came to the throne of God in prayer and praise. As in my sabbatical times at home, this worship time filled me with peace. My thoughts turned from the words of the songs to just praising God from my heart. My body danced a little while I praised. Others down front were much more demonstrative in their dancing, but it wasn't a contest. I reminded myself that even after all these years, I was still a recovering Methodist.

Minutes turned into an hour. When I occasionally opened my eyes between songs, I saw that many more people had joined the thirty or so who had been in the basement at the beginning of the praise time. A man up front who looked like Snoop Dogg bounced up and down, praising the Lord enthusiastically; his dreadlocks bounced in rhythm with the music. My faith became sight as I realized again that the gospel was for everyone, even ones who looked much different than what I was used to at first glance. It wasn't for any one culture or race. Jesus was God's gift to all men and women, and we were all equal in His sight. Some preferred loud rock, others bluegrass or soul, but worship was all about our ability to use music to praise God. It was all about Him.

Another song began, and the leader encouraged everyone to dance before the Lord. King David in the Bible danced before the Lord so fervently that he embarrassed his wife. She didn't like to see him strip off his royal robes and dance in minimal clothing like the commoners. She told him, "You're the king of the whole country—why are you embarrassing yourself?" He responded with something to the effect of, "You ain't seen nothin' yet. I'm really going to embarrass you now, because it's about the Lord, not me or you."

That's how I felt. I wasn't sure if my business friends or some of my more reserved Christian friends would have liked it. But it was all about Jesus and no one else. As I danced a little more, the glory of the Lord became visible in my mind. I could see the long white train of Jesus' garment billow down from His throne and through the ceiling of the room I was in. The scripture came to me, "If I can just touch the hem of His garment, I will be made whole." I raised my hands as high as I could, and both my hands felt the hem of Jesus' garment. I worshiped the Lord as I felt His healing power flow into my body. I became well in ways I'd never imagined. Joy flooded through my mind and body. It was as if I was reborn again. Deep fears left me and have never returned. Worries about the future melted away and never came back with the same intensity. It was a transformational night in many ways.

I loved the song by Savage Garden that said "I knew I loved you before I met you." It probably wasn't written about God, but it reminded me of His love for me. God knew me before He created me, and He loved me even then.

That night I walked out of that church basement deeply healed in body, mind, and soul. I'm not sure why God cared enough about me to invite me to a basement on a Saturday night, but He knew how much I needed it. Thank God that I had heard Him through my body's self-indulgent whining for a night at home in front of the television saying, "Come away with Me."

The Goodness of God

While these adventures were beautiful and amazing, I looked forward more and more to the adventure of one day being in heaven as I continued learning and allowing my fears to drop away. In the book of Revelation in the Bible, John wrote about the marriage supper of the Lamb, a future event when those who had accepted Christ would sit down to a huge celebratory meal. This meal would be better than the Super Bowl, Christmas, and the Fourth of July all in one. As I relished the growing peace and joy I was finding in my sabbatical, I grew increasingly confident of this future adventure that would eclipse all others.

At one time in my life I had known nothing about heaven, so I had asked God to give me a vision of the afterlife. God answered my prayer not long after my dad's death.

I was sleeping in on a Saturday morning and missing my daddy very much. Suddenly I was at the marriage supper of the Lamb. The table stretched out of sight in both directions, farther than I could see. Everything was incredibly beautiful. The other dinner guests seemed familiar to me, but I didn't immediately recognize them. I looked down at my white plate with ornate gold borders—and something amazing caught my eye.

Each piece of silverware was gold. The stem of each knife, fork, and spoon was engraved with the name of the person to be seated at that place setting. My name was on my silverware! I was so excited. Jesus had taken time to put each person's names on his or her pieces of silverware! I wanted to tell the person next to me about this amazing discovery. Surely he would be just as floored by the revelation.

"Hey, look! Our names are on our silverware," I said excitedly to the man.

"I guess they are," he calmly replied.

Wow, how could this guy not even acknowledge something right before our faces? I thought. But wait a minute. That was exactly what my dad used to say. Right then I knew it was him. My father was seated right next to me. And my mother and brother were across from us. They all looked so incredibly young. Each of them was in a beautiful glorified state, their faces glowing to a point that I couldn't look directly into their eyes.

I woke up knowing that heaven existed. I'm not sure why a dream about my father made me so sure that heaven was real, but it did. God knew how much I needed to know for sure right at that moment in my life. With my anchor, my dad, having departed this world for the next, I felt adrift. God wanted me to find my anchor in Him.

That was really the story of my sabbatical too. I had left work to find God again. While I had never doubted my faith after returning to the Lord, I had gotten a little lost in the middle of my everyday life. Church activity, work, friends, busyness—they had all caused me to lose my way. In several short months off, I had found my way again.

Church Change

The merger that prompted my decision to resign from being an Elder eventually neared. I decided that the resulting entity would not be the right church home for me. Unlike previous church changes, it didn't take much thought to know where I was going next. I'd already built relationships with several people at Capital Baptist Church. The strong Biblical teaching and warm personalities there led me like a beacon to their shore.

It was sad to say goodbye to the few close friends that remained at my former church. With so many who had already gone, there weren't too many left—but they were survivors and fellow warriors like myself. During all the hard times, we had stuck together and now I was just one more friend to say a temporary goodbye to them. We would all see each other at an event here or there, but our time of close fellowship was over. This hurt me all over again, not just for my personal pain, but also the thought of making their journey even slightly more difficult.

21

ME, MOVIE STAR

THE POST ON FACEBOOK STOOD OUT like an ice-cream cone on a hot day. After all the wonderful days of my sabbatical, it was hard to imagine anything better happening, but God had saved the best for last. I read that my friend, Robin Osborn, was helping a sister church that was hosting a movie-production company to film in our area. My heart sped up, and I started to smile. Acting in a movie had been a thirty-year-old prayer of mine. Could I get up the courage to try out for a part?

For the last ten years, I had written, produced, and directed our church's Christmas productions. My scripts were quirky and usually funny. I often kept a small part for myself, especially since it was hard to get men to act. This amateur hour hardly qualified me to try out for a movie, but the opportunity couldn't be missed. My last real acting gig had been in high school, when I had played Lazar Wolf in *Fiddler on the Roof*. Somehow I didn't think Hollywood would be impressed. But what did I have to lose? Maybe I could be an extra or something.

One of the requirements for applying included an eight-by-ten head shot. I decided to go to Sears and see what they could do. After balking at paying six times more than advertised on their website, I decided that a buddy of mine could take my picture. The photos made me look as if I had a five o'clock shadow; perhaps I could be cast as a tough guy or a former alcoholic. My friend assured me that I didn't look that bad, so I loaded the pictures onto my computer, and in an instant, my application was sent.

Several days passed, and the phone finally rang. It was someone from the movie. When could I come for an audition? My heart beat fast again. How many people actually get to audition for a movie?

Suddenly I realized that the movie would probably be shooting after I went back to work, assuming I did indeed get back to work. Hopefully I could get a few hours off—if I was fortunate enough to get a part.

Trying Out

On Friday I drove around the Beltway to the Northern Virginia suburbs. As I neared the location, suddenly I felt that I might slide back into a panic attack. This movie thing was a bad idea. I called a friend and spit out my problem in eight seconds or less. "I signed up for an audition for a movie, and I can't do it. I'm feeling just as nuts as when I was working for the government. What am I going to do?"

My friend started slowly. "You don't have to do it—if you don't want to." This was brilliant. His words took the pressure off. "But if this is a lifelong dream of yours, wouldn't it be better to give it a try and fail?" He kept talking, but I didn't need to hear anymore. He was right. I'd always dreamed of entertaining people. How could I not go—even if I did have a heart attack and die trying? Most likely, though, I knew I would be sitting safely in my sunroom in a few hours knowing that I'd done the best I could do.

When I arrived, I discovered an old friend working in the building where the auditions were being held. He came out of his office and hugged me, and I felt worlds better. It was amazing to me that God had arranged to have this friend nearby during the audition. I explained to my friend why I was there, and he patted me on the back and told me to break a leg. I went upstairs, and an assistant showed me into the registration room. Someone gave me some paperwork to sign, and someone else took a new head shot of me. The one I had sent was not adequate. (What a waste of time that had been.)

Soon I was called for the screen test. All the adult male actors were reading lines from the movie's lead role. The director, Donald Leow, took my resume and newly minted head shot and introduced himself and his assistant producer, Cortney Matz. About ten seconds later, the cameraman was ready. "Action," Donald said. (How cool was that? A real director had said "Action" to me. I could barely contain my excitement.) I read the part with a person offstage reading the opposite part. Donald had me read a second time, and then he asked me what kind of part I wanted. I explained that I was looking for something small but would help in any way he wanted me to. I just wanted to be part of the project.

"Would you mind studying some lines and reading for a couple other parts?" Donald asked me. "If you have time today, we could do it now."

Oh, I had time, all right.

Donald's wife, Saundra, ushered me back into the registration room. She found the appropriate lines and gave me some encouragement. Saundra reminded me of Yoko Ono. She was extremely quiet and more than a little intriguing.

I went back in front of the camera, even though I didn't have the lines fully memorized. One of the roles was a pastor at a funeral; the other was a congressman. Donald was patient with my lack of memorization. At the end of the audition, he smiled. "You will be the congressman, I think, although I'll have to check with the producers to be sure. I'll call you."

My head swam again. I thanked him profusely and headed back to my car. This was the craziest thing I'd ever done, and somehow it was working. It looked like I was going to get an actual part in an actual movie. The funny thing is that I had managed hundreds of millions of dollars in my day job, but this movie thing was much more exciting to me.

I quickly called a friend and my mom to tell them the good news.

Rehearsal

A few days passed, and I tried not to be too disappointed that the movie people had not called. Then one afternoon, out of the blue, Donald was on the phone. Yes, it was a good time to talk, I told him. No, I wouldn't mind having two scenes in the movie. Yes, I could come for a read-through with the rest of the cast on a Saturday six weeks from now.

I hung up the phone and floated up to cloud nine. I had a small part, but I couldn't have been happier if I'd gotten the lead in a Broadway musical opposite Kristin Chenoweth. I had a bunch of details to take care of before the read-through—doing more paperwork, figuring out wardrobe, making sure I had a day job.

Finally the day of the read-through arrived. Since this was a small-budget movie, two of the leads wouldn't be there, but the female lead was. Nancy Fondriest was amazing. She played the alcoholic mom of a future Olympic soccer player. Boy, could she act! I was in awe of how good everyone was. I'd not been around professional actors before. It was energizing. I friended everyone who would have me on Facebook.

We did a couple team-building exercises, read the first half of the script, and had lunch. A friend of mine, Fred Kory, had also landed a small acting part—the pastor role that I had also read for. I knew Fred from our church plays. He and his wife, Judy, and I ate lunch together. It was fun to catch up with them and share the movie experience with someone I knew.

As I read my lines that day, I received several positive comments from the younger cast members. "You really nailed that congressman role," someone told me. Praise—it was beyond my comprehension that someone in this group had thought I'd done well. How crazy to hear positive feedback when I couldn't believe I was even doing a movie.

My First Day on Set

The following Saturday I drove up to the suburban office building where we would be filming. Someone led me to the breakfast area under some tents. A man in an apron was cooking eggs, and a few boxes of cereal sat on the tables. The food was not great, but I didn't care. It was movie food!

I was ushered into the building where the shooting would soon begin. It was so cool to see all the people, cameras, lights, microphones. Two of the lead actors who were in my scene introduced themselves. Jason Burkey, the male lead, was a rising star. The actor who played his father, Michael Landers sat down with me at a table to kill time.

I quickly learned that actors tend to stick together on set and production people tend to have their own group. Actors came and went from day to day, but the production people stayed together the entire filming, so they tended to bond.

I learned so much from my fellow actors. They talked about how they had gotten roles, about the challenges of making enough money acting, and about how much they liked our director. Apparently all directors were not as great to work with as Donald—they liked him very much. Making a Christian movie was no doubt different than working on a secular film, but it strengthened my faith to work with real men of God who were also kind.

My turn for makeup arrived. The makeup guy had worked on hundreds of movies. He thought my hair was perfect, which I found humorous because I had so little of it. He applied a layer of foundation on my ample jowls and highlighted my features. Fortunately I didn't need a lot of lipstick, as I'm sure I would have eaten that off after a few minutes.

The associate producer called for us to come on set. In this first scene I was supposed to walk out of an office with the power-hungry dad and meet the soccer-playing son, Jason Burkey. I would say a couple of lines, and then I was supposed to turn and exit.

We rehearsed the scene once, and then we shot it.

The assistant director asked for a second take because the lighting hadn't been right the first time. This time, after saying my lines, I turned right to exit and discovered a large lighting stand in my path. I clumsily hopped over it and exited.

The director, watching the scene on a computer in the next room, asked for another take, so we shot it again with some minor change he wanted. Perhaps he would like me not hopping like a kangaroo. This time I thought I would get creative and turn to my left so I wouldn't have to hop over the lighting stand.

The reaction was immediate. "Cut!" Someone yelled. "He turned the opposite way. You have to turn to your right, Senator."

"He's a congressman."

"Whatever he is, he has to turn the same way every time if we hope to edit this."

I turned red, and we rewound the scene. Eventually everyone was happy, and we moved on to the next scene. I loved the movie talk. When he yelled, "Quiet on the set!" I almost wet myself. When they go from one seen to another, the assistant director would yell, "Moving On." This was the dream of a lifetime.

It was time to wait some more. Though my scene was over, we all had to stay around in case re-shoots were required. Twila Ilgenfritz, a beautiful blonde actress with a great sense of humor, came to talk with me as we sat waiting. She and I laughed and talked to the point of getting shushed once by a production assistant. She explained several tips for getting acting work in the Washington area and told me a few of the highlights of her career.

After an hour or so, we were told that the sound had been bad in the office where we had shot my scene. We would need to go into a different office and rerecord the sound. It would be dubbed in later. It was kind of fun to have the chance to read the same lines with slightly different inflection each time. After rerecording, we wrapped for the day at that location, and I was allowed to leave.

I learned that day that acting was indeed work. There was also a lot of waiting around and goofing off when it wasn't one's turn. It took a whole lot of people to make a movie.

Humor on the Set

Several days later, my second scene was more robust as well as more challenging. I was to be a guest at a big party at the power-hungry dad's suburban mansion. The party scene was beautiful, and the other guests included a few real-life friends of mine from the area that I knew from church.

I showed up way early, as requested, and then waited four hours to begin shooting. The challenging thing, as we gathered in the parlor and dining room for the filming, is that the air condition- ing was not on. It being a typical muggy early summer evening in Virginia, I began to sweat almost immediately. Fortunately I had brought three shirts that looked exactly the same. In the scene the boozy wife (Nancy Fondriest) was to spill a drink on my congress- man character. She had to spill it well, as this was the catalyst for a juicy fight that she would have with her hubby as soon as the party guests cleared out.

Finally we shot the scene. I sweated a lot. Nancy spilled her drink on me. Then all of us guests left the party. We stood for a few minutes outside the front door in front of hot lights, and then we went back in for another take.

This created the scenario for a huge comedy sequence between scenes. As soon as I'd had the drink spilled on me and had left the party, I jumped over the hedge. I ripped off my shirt, and wardrobe handed me another, which I quickly put on. The continuity person checked to make sure I looked the same. Then I jumped back over the hedge and went in through the front door. We repeated the scene about six times, and since I had only three shirts, wardrobe had to blow-dry one of my shirts between each take. I wished the camera could have been outside—it was funnier than anything I'd seen on film in a while. Come to think of it, I wasn't sure I wanted my bare chest out there for all to see.

Eventually our long night ended. I had an hour-plus drive back to Maryland from this far-out Virginia suburb. My contact lenses stuck to eyes due to my makeup, and sweat made it worse. When I got home after one in the morning, I was exhausted—and thoroughly hooked on the movie business.

A Dream Come True

When filming ended a couple weeks later, we had a wrap party. It was great to have a chance say goodbye to the other actors and the director and producer.

Being in this movie made my dream a reality, and for that I would be eternally grateful to Donald and Sandra Leow, Chris Rogers (the executive producer), and the many fine Christian actors who shared a hot month in Virginia. After filming wrapped, I continued to get a window into the Christian film business via friendship with Rich Swingle. He is crazy talented and constantly on the road acting and teaching acting to others who want to change the world through film and stage plays.

I got to see the movie, *For the Glory*, with about five hundred other people in a big theater some months later at the Virginia premiere. I loved seeing it with a large crowd and felt so thankful when the director asked all the actors to stand afterward. I'd taken the sabbatical to focus on the "big four" and to pursue a bonus desire of fulfilling a few dreams, and now God had blessed me beyond my wildest imaginings. My bucket list had one less item now.

22

PREPARING FOR A
NEW BEGINNING

ABOUT FOUR MONTHS into my sabbatical of the mind I started thinking seriously about coming back to work. It wasn't that I didn't like the sabbatical, it was my love of eating and driving a car and living in a house or apartment. About a month after the Army interview, I had two more, one with NASA and one with the Nuclear Regulatory Agency. Each time I thought that I had the job and each time I was disappointed with a rejection letter. When I reached out for feedback, they both had internal candidates that knew more about their specific practices within the Agencies. While I fought feelings that age discrimination may have played a part, God told me to hang on and not worry.

One morning, I felt prompted to call my old boss at the three-letter Agency and get specific about coming back. While he had told me that I could come back, Government requires paperwork to make anything official. He wasn't in, but called me back later in the morning. Suspecting the reason for my call, he had already gotten permission from his boss to formally offer me a job. When I got off the phone, I nearly fell dancing around my house. It was so exciting to know that someone wanted me, that God had a plan all along. What better place to go than someplace where everything would be familiar?

Five months earlier I had started my sabbatical wondering if I was going crazy. I had even feared that life might be winding down for me, that my days for dreaming and adventuring had come to an end. I had constantly feared death. But no! God wasn't finished with this middle-aged, creative-minded, slightly humorous con- tracting worker. He had more for me to do. My sabbatical was not an ending—it was a new beginning.

Five months off work—what had it accomplished? Had I found my peace again? Yes, I had, and I had found a renewed sense of purpose too. But now all this was about to be put to the test as I prepared to return to work.

Planning for Peace

Prior to my sabbatical, I had been worn out, tired, and not well physically or psychologically. While I hadn't been a raving lunatic, I had played one at work and at church on occasion (and that definitely wasn't the kind of acting I had always dreamed of doing). Now I needed to think about how I wanted to live as I returned to the daily work routine.

Could I handle Monday mornings? Angry customers? Unhappy employees? Strangely, I thought I could. I sure didn't want to stay on sabbatical permanently—that would have been boring. God had formed me perfectly to play a role in taking care of people and the rest of His creation. I wanted to do my part toward making the world a better place for my fellow travelers.

One of the keys to maintaining my peace as I returned to work would be making sure that I lived differently than I had before the sabbatical. This would require some planning. I didn't want to get back to work and find myself in the same old rat race. I had put a lot of effort into dealing with the big four areas of life—physical, emotional, spiritual, and financial—by changing my diabetes meds, increasing my physical exercise, eating better, getting my church commitments under control, spending time in study and prayer, and paying off debts. I didn't want to lose the gains I'd made. To keep this from happening, I needed to adopt a new schedule—daily, weekly, and monthly routines.

The first priority had to be spiritual. Spiritually speaking, my sabbatical had been like a five-month retreat; it had given me a renewed commitment to serving God and learning more through living life. As I returned to work, time for daily prayer and meditation would be a must. I needed a director for my new adventure, and God was the only One capable of success at directing a human life. The calendar had to be mastered to create pockets of rest when I would stop and receive replenishment from the Holy Spirit. During my sabbatical I had found what fed my heart and soul; now I needed to plan it into my life as I went back to work.

The physical would be the most difficult for me. This had been an area of struggle throughout my life. My use of food and exercise was the area I'd been least willing to give God control over. In my younger years it had been about rebellion and self-comforting; over the years it had become more about weakness and lack of discipline.

Steve Reynold's book *Bod 4 God* had done a great job of explaining to me the battle between my wants for temporary happiness and my need for long-term health. Would I choose short-term satisfaction, or would I choose a lifetime of feeling better, being more productive for the Lord, and living longer for myself and those I loved? I was still involved as a leader with my Losing to Live weight-loss team at church. Although my flesh wanted to stop concentrating on exercise and healthy eating, with diabetes a part of my life, it was no time for me to give up on my physical health.

Letting God take control of my finances had been easy. Money had never been my main concern in life, and I had not been a big success when it came to financial matters. Generally I had spent most of what I'd received and then some. The sabbatical had helped me relearn what I already knew: debt was bondage.

One of my financial goals now as I returned to the agency was to be able to leave government service close to my minimum retirement age. This would allow me to concentrate after retirement on other things like writing and producing Christian-themed projects. To make this happen, I needed to nix the debt and save a substantial nest egg. The sabbatical had given me some of the tools to be able to do that. Now my budget was based on reality instead of pie in the sky. I had a plan for all funds that didn't go toward a bill. God would be part of my daily planning for finances and for the future.

Emotionally the sabbatical had been hard for me in some ways. Even though I had enjoyed good times with several friends, at times I had felt isolated. Some friends wondered what I was doing quitting my job, and I sensed some of them backing away from me during the sabbatical. Of course, maybe they were just super busy with their lives.

Looking forward, however, I realized that I would actually feel more comfortable being back at work when it came to the area of emotions. It had been peaceful and calm at home, but people energized me. It would be great to be back at work and exercise my ability to meet and become friends with people. Human beings were the crowning achievement of creation, and I prayed that I would not only see the beauty in human complexity and potential but that God would use me in new ways to minister to the people who surrounded me at work.

Change Is Possible

Was all this change really possible, though? After all, I had made all my gains in an optimal environment. Could I really continue these changes in my life after I went back to work?

I could only fall back on prior experience of growth in my life to help me answer that question.

One of my earliest self-realizations was that my sense of humor was not like everyone else's. For example, as an eight-year-old, I liked playing at a friend's house. One day my friend annoyed me on purpose with some silly antic. A short time later, he informed me that he needed to go in the house and use the bathroom. I easily persuaded him not to go to all that trouble—he could just go behind the front bush, and no one could see him from the street. No sooner had he begun to do his business than I ran in the house and told his mother that he was whizzing in the bushes. In fact, she could see him from the large picture window if she just moved a little closer to it. She came outside and scolded him and then thanked me for bringing this to her attention. I decided it was time to go home. As I skipped along, I laughed and laughed about the prank I had just pulled. I thought it was hilarious, but nobody else did.

My odd sense of humor became a defense mechanism, and for years I laughed whenever I got nervous. This caused problems, however, when someone mistook my laughter for a lack of concern at his anger or pain. God and life helped me overcome this behavior by teaching me that it was okay for people to get upset. It was okay for people to be wounded. The world would not end if another person felt negative emotions. Whether it was me or something else that had caused the person to feel badly, it was better to respond appropriately than to laugh. Progress!

Change was possible. Even if I had deeply ingrained patterns of behavior, I could change for the better. Although it doesn't sound like a revelation, it was something I needed to relearn. Mental pathways can be re-shaped with determination.

God wanted me to become better each day I lived. He didn't want me to do it by striving for perfection, as the world does; rather, He simply wanted me to accept His help in the process of living my life. I had started to depend on the tools at my disposal—the Bible, prayer, the Holy Spirit, other people—to help me move from anxious mess to more relaxed Christian. I could go from useless in my anxious busyness to useful as I rested in God's perfect peace.

If I concentrated on God, He would bring the changes I needed in my life. Returning to work would be a test to find out how much I'd changed during my sabbatical. The accuser told me that I hadn't moved forward, but I refused to listen. Even when my progress slowed, I would press on in faith, no matter what. In twenty-five years I didn't want to be the same person I was now. All that began with getting back to work.

I was a little anxious about jumping back onto the merry-go-round of Washington life with all its craziness, busyness, confusion, and challenges. But Jesus showed His disciples what to do with their fears. He would show me what to do when confronted with a pickpocket on the Metro subway train. The disciples, as they were tossed in a terrible storm at sea, fretted that their boat would be lost. Jesus, however, calmly slept. His disciples woke Him up and anxiously informed Him of their "dire" situation. Although He scolded them for their lack of faith, I wonder if He smiled inside because He knew what He was going to do: "He arose, and rebuked the wind, and said unto the sea, Peace, be still. And the wind ceased, and there was a great calm" (Mark 4:39). With just a word from Jesus, the storm was over. Great calm came over the disciples' world in an instant. It was the courage I now possessed.

My heart and mind had been changed over the past five months because the One who could stop the storms of life with just a few words had worked His healing power in my life. I could confidently live my life out in the real world because Jesus would hear my prayers; He was standing at the ready to save me.

23

New Peace, New Purpose

MY FIRST MORNING COMMUTING BACK TO WORK, I drove the city streets heading for the orientation site. Even though I'd been away for only five-plus months, personnel required me go back through the full two-day orientation. For the most part I didn't mind, but the orientation would be held on the twelfth floor of a glass building that features a large center atrium. As a life-long acrophobic in recovery, this was my least favorite building in the three-letter-agency's arsenal.

Though the change in my diabetes medication had greatly improved my condition, I was still not eager to test my ability to handle high places. Throughout my life this phobia had waxed and waned—but mostly waxed. On my way to work that first day, I started feeling anxious about the building. I pulled off on a side street and parked. With the motor running, I got out of my Impala to pray. This is where the rubber met the road in more ways than one.

The cold air and prayer helped pull me out of the "what ifs" and back into the moment. Perhaps this was the real beginning of the test to see how far the sabbatical has really brought me. It might have been a temptation to give up and go home. But that wouldn't work. Jesus and I had come too far in the past months. Besides, I needed the money.

Climbing back into my car, I knew God was with me.

I arrived at the attractive newer-looking building about fifteen minutes later. My heart ticked up a notch as I waited for the elevator. As the doors opened on the twelfth floor, I felt a little woozy. Courage (and a desire to eat the continental breakfast that would be offered) pushed me out of the elevator. My friend the Holy Spirit told me that I could get right back on that elevator if I couldn't stand it. It was true—I could go downstairs anytime I wanted. My feet moved quickly to the large desk backing up to the glass atrium. My eyes stayed focused on the receptionist's desk and impeccable manicured hands. The woman checked my name and told me to walk down the enclosed stairwell to the training rooms below. I knew the drill from previous training in the building. The training rooms were down a floor, connected by a well-adorned, interior stairwell. Only those with a special key card could get to the 11th floor without going through the receptionist on the twelfth. It was so wonderful to move away from the view of the center atrium and descend, even one floor.

The training rooms came into view as I descended, and I found a seat facing away from the bank of windows that opened to the atrium. In seconds I was relaxed and chatting with the other new employees. I reflected with gratitude on the strength I'd gained during my sabbatical journey.

The presentations were well organized, the presenters having given them hundreds and hundreds of times. Thankfully, this held my attention most of the time. The fact that my seat faced away from the windows also helped me focus. As an added show of His care for me, God moved someone to close the blinds so that we could see the slide projector better. I was pleased. It was an uncomfortable day at times, but God helped me through it. I had gone from the safety and security of my couch to perils of a twelve-story building.

A New Sense of Purpose

As I settled into my new job, I was quickly reminded that life wasn't a perpetual retreat. People had moments that were less than serene, that was for sure. It made me sad that first week to see how everyone treated each other in a typical office environment. It wasn't blatant meanness I saw but pain and fear running under the surface of so . many people's lives. Many walked around with hurts and grudges, leading them to hurt others with their reactions to everyday situations. Sometimes I felt as if I were drowning in my co-workers' and customers' dysfunctions. I remembered this feeling from the aftermath of Christian retreats and conferences I had attended. Times away with the Lord remind me how far the human race is from the perfection God intended.

But one of the reasons God had brought me back to work was to love my employees and bring a little bit of that peace with me. During my sabbatical I had thought and prayed about what it meant to use my talents for God, and He had led me right here, back to my government job. While I wasn't perfectly healed of all my anxiety, I was refreshed and renewed, and the peace I had found while resting in God's presence in my quiet sunroom had cleared away the cobwebs and prepared me for serving God in useful and effective ways.

Life, I had to remember, was not about me. It was about God. I was not the center of my universe—God was. My petty fears didn't compare to His awesome splendor. If I would trust Him, I could participate with Him as He cared for the people in my world. My life could have meaning as I loved others on behalf of their heavenly Father.

The people I worked with, like all people everywhere, needed bosses and authority figures who genuinely love them. They needed people who were on their side, wanting them to succeed. They needed role models who didn't take things too seriously yet demonstrated the covering that God intended authority figures to provide. When they did wrong, employees needed leaders who would be willing to tell them so but who would also be quick to forgive. A good boss was actually a gift from God to an employee. If I could listen to my employees, I could help them move forward in their jobs and in life.

My work went from an exercise in futility to a platform for God's miracles. The focus of my career changed from climbing the corporate ladder to nurturing, teaching, coaching, loving, and directing my employees and co-workers. If I let it, life could be a big adventure. But I had to leave my fears behind to go on this adventure. I had to surrender each day to the inevitable eternity of God. As I did, I was able to greet each new morning with expectation. I had endless possibilities as I sought to love my friends, family, neighbors, co-workers, and even my enemies.

For many years I had separated my work life and my Christian life. Church was church, and work was work. Then in 2003 I learned when I got my MBA at Regent University that my work mattered to God. My place of work could be my ministry—the very place where God wanted to work out His purpose through me to take care of people. Now I remembered to pray about meetings and about people at work. Like anyone, I wasn't perfect, and I sometimes offended others, but now I knew how to say I was sorry and ask for forgiveness. I tried to honor God with my behavior and decisions at work.

Fighting Battles in Prayer

I was thrilled to be back at the agency with a calm heart and a fresh vision. But I was reminded pretty quickly that I had an enemy who wanted to make life difficult and bring me down. Generally I knew I was in a spiritual battle when a conflict didn't make sense. Thankfully, I knew what the Bible taught about facing enemies who were more than flesh and blood: my strength didn't lie in earthly, carnal weapons but in spiritual weapons. Whenever I came up against something greater than an ordinary human problem, my Father wanted me to bring the issue to Him.

One of my favorite miracles involves a time when I was unhappy in a job. My boss and I were not getting along. She was a different personality type from me, and I couldn't understand why she got under my skin so much. Everything she did irritated me, and vice versa. So I began to pray for a new job.

But even though God had helped me get jobs before, I struggled to believe that He could and would do it again. It wasn't that I thought He couldn't do it; I was more worried that He didn't love me enough to answer my prayer. I felt unworthy to receive anything from Him (and I was). But I still asked Him.

I sat moping one day at a small office party with my cake and punch. The big boss of the organization came and sat next to me. She said that she had heard I wasn't happy in my job. After getting over my embarrassment, I tried to make light of my unhappiness. But the big boss invited me to come see her the next morning, which I did. She offered me a couple other jobs in the organization but told me to take some time and think them over. Next she had her deputy send my resume out to several other divisions of our organization. Eventually I received seven job offers. I selected the best one and happily moved on.

In the wake of that job change, I praised God for His miraculous provision. I also got up in front of my whole church and told them how God had blessed me.

At times in my life I hadn't kept praying until the answer came, but now, if I wanted to keep living in God's peace and love my employees and other co-workers, I had to learn to do spiritual battle. And when God did miracles for me, I needed to get down on my knees and thank Him for His kindness to an old sinner. Then I needed to tell someone else. Thank You, Jesus. Thank You, Lord.

24

FINDING LASTING PEACE

CORETTA, SAL, AND TANISHA wandered into my office actively discussing the issue of the moment. I looked up from an e-mail I'd been writing and smiled at them. They felt no trepidation or fear of disturbing me; the trio meandered in and plopped down, knowing that I would rather spend time with people than with my computer anytime. "Is now a good time to talk with you?" Coretta asked.

As I warmly welcomed these three employees, I thought back to the pre-sabbatical me. In my fifty years of life before my sabbatical, peace had been elusive. Oh, I had enjoyed interludes of contentment, but I did not have a permanent and lasting peace.

During my sabbatical I had learned to go to the source of God's peace when earthly peace started to evaporate: "Great peace have they which love thy law; and nothing shall offend them" (Ps. 119:165). Spending time in God's Word had changed me to the point at which I was much less easily offended. That, I thought, was wonderful.

Colossians 3:15 had given me particular insight into having and keeping peace: I needed to "let the peace of God rule in [my] heart." In other words, I had to do my part to let peace in. Running around like crazy from five in the morning until eight at night and getting home dog tired and woofing too much food and going to bed hadn't allowed the peace of God to rule in my heart; setting aside time for daily prayer and meditation did.

A Full Life

Abundant life as promised by Jesus in the Bible was more than just existing. It was more than conquering fear with difficulty every step of the way. Real life was about doing everything that God had planned for me each day. It meant going on the offensive. It meant reaching out and grabbing those things that God wanted for me and for those on my path. It was about love, peace, freedom from fear. It was about paying so much attention to helping others that I forgot myself and my selfish desires.

God intended me to have freedom from pain, disease, and mental torment. When the fallen state of our world interfered and illness or injury found its way into my circumstances, I had an advocate in Jesus. When the doctor didn't have any good news, I could go to the Father via the Son and plead for mercy. I could find wellness again. Second Peter 1:2 told me how: "Grace and peace be multiplied unto you through the knowledge of God, and of Jesus our Lord." Knowing God and Jesus and focusing on truth would increase my peace.

I had found freedom. I had a rested feeling that energized me. Suddenly I could leap tall spiritual buildings with a single bound.

With an enlarged vision of the future, I would now be able to accomplish more with the time I had left. God didn't intend for me to sit down and retire from life. He had given me renewed strength to tackle the future with assurance that He was right there with me. "If God be for us, who can be against us?" (Rom. 8:31).

New Perspective

After my initial trepidation at the orientation meetings, I settled back into normal. My stress level was much lower than it had been before, and the pace of my new office was much slower than the one I'd left. My fear stayed at bay most of the time, and I began enjoying being back at work.

I also discovered again that people were generally God's coolest creation. I experienced an endless supply of interesting twists in managing people. My perspective had changed 180 degrees. I was back at work to love my staff and take care of them. It was about God and others—not about me.

Stopping for a sabbatical had given me a new perspective on life. By learning to understand the blessings of each season of my life—whether I was on sabbatical or back at work—I had learned to make the most of each one. The trick was to live in the moment and the day. I was going to squeeze every opportunity that came my way for all the life it would provide.

This wasn't the same as busyness—being driven and stressed out by people and circumstances. It was enjoying the people, places, and things that God provided for the moment. As I came at my job from this angle, I began to cultivate in my life the riches that impressed God: "love, joy, peace, longsuffering, gentleness, goodness, faith, meekness, temperance" (Gal. 5:22–23). As I walked in the Spirit of God, I watched the fruit of the Spirit develop in my life.

Perhaps I was now a little more patient and willing to listen to others. Maybe I was in less of a hurry than I had been before. Peace followed me into the office each day and preceded me in difficult tasks. I had a new appreciation for opportunities that I hadn't seen before I slowed down and tried to listen to God.

My sabbatical was not an ending but a beginning to more life. It had vividly taught me that I couldn't run through life at a hundred miles an hour and expect to hear from God or make wise choices. I needed to regularly slow down and pray.

During my time away, as I had read the thoughts of many other people in their books and on their websites, I had learned a thing or two. Surprise—other people had a lot of great things to say! Humility reminded me that I didn't have all the answers. God wanted to give me answers and the guidance I needed to maximize my time. He wanted me to have abundant life every day.

To receive something good, sometimes we have to empty our plate to make room for it. The new me learned not to jump at every possible activity; sometimes I needed to be home on the couch reading a book. I divested some responsibilities and took on some different ones.

A New Me

My mind came back to Coretta, Sal, and Tanisha. The issue at hand was not a technical one but a people problem. A difficult customer was pushing to speed up a procurement. Unfortunately, what the customer wanted did not match the paperwork she had written up and signed, and she flatly refused to adjust the write-up.

Sal explained how the customer's write-up was weak and had multiple discrepancies. "I feel like I'm wearing out," he told me. "She says she won't do another write-up. If I don't use what she's written, she's threatening to go to our boss."

I asked several questions to be sure I understood the situation and felt confident that each of my employees had done their jobs correctly. As my employees spoke comfortably for thirty minutes, I smiled at how far all of us had come. They had learned to trust me, even to feel comfortable enough to stroll into my office sans appointment without fear of being brushed off. I'd learned to slow down and focus on what they were saying and not on my next appointment. It's not that the pressure had gone away—it just didn't have the same impact as before.

"Here's what I suggest," I told them. "We have to make every effort to work with this customer. If we just tell her no, this ball will be back in our court in a week or so. Let's offer to sit with her staffer and do one more draft. Then we submit the package to legal and let them talk to her if they aren't satisfied."

I was different. The shouts and deadlines and honking horns were the same, but my ears had been trained to care more about the feelings coming out of my employees' hearts than the words coming out of their mouths. Of course our work was important, and we couldn't compromise on the final results, but the way we got there didn't have to be a road paved with stress, acrimony, and character assassination. We could all be at peace—and find real results, even for the person who was causing the problem.

As they left my office, I leaned back and smiled. If someone had walked past my door and glanced into my office just then, they would not have known why I sat at my desk with a Cheshire-cat-like grin across my face. But I knew what God had done in one life. My sabbatical had made me a different person. I now saw the end result, and it was a happy one.

Afterword

I have no idea where my life might have gone if I hadn't taken a sabbatical. My five months off work offered me opportunities that don't happen every day (for me, anyway): reading twenty-five books, trying out for a movie and getting a part, following a niece to Walt Disney World and watching her compete in her first marathon, taking an eighteen-hour train ride on an overnight trip, and deciding to change churches. The inertia of everyday life wouldn't have allowed me time to take the slow train to Florida or the energy to leave a bunch of friends at one church to join another.

It also seemed miraculous to me that several weeks into the sabbatical I was able to do things that had once caused fear and now have no debilitating reaction. I still didn't want to go for a balloon ride, but I felt much safer walking around the balcony of a favorite restaurant—something I hadn't been able to do months before.

While discontinuing Actos may or may not be the reason my fear subsided, it had to have been a factor, based on the results of the change. Of course, I'd also quit working a couple weeks earlier and was deliberately de-stressing my life, and I had also stopped drinking Diet Pepsi. In short, other factors besides Actos had probably contributed to my panic attacks. Whatever they were, however, it was great to have the panic attacks all but a distant memory. The good news is that the attacks did not recur when I returned to work. Whatever their exact cause, God used the sabbatical time to get them out of my life. (I'm still afraid of high places though.)

After the sabbatical ended, the gains I had made in the big four areas of life during my time off work continued. Physically I ended up in better shape. My walking habit endured and even increased after I went back to work, and I found that even twenty minutes per day devoted to walking made me feel much better physically. The gym remained in my life as well. My weight even went down a few pounds after the sabbatical, though I still have a long way to go.

Several things I didn't get around to during my sabbatical. It would have been great to have joined a recreational volleyball league, take an entry-level aerobics class, or hike the Appalachian Trail, to name a few things. I guess I needed to save something for retirement.

I gained emotionally by having new social opportunities on my sabbatical. I invited a number of friends over for dinner, although I didn't invite someone every week as I had originally hoped to do. And I finally met my neighbors! After the sabbatical I didn't put as much thought into my emotional well-being, aka my social life, as I could have. Mainly this was because I had plenty of people contact in my job. My close friends and I went out to dinner at about the right intervals for me, as well, so I have generally been content with social interactions.

The financial lessons I learned from my sabbatical were many. Dave Ramsey provided me a lot of commonsense advice in his books. Finances, he wrote, were about long-term success versus short-term satisfaction. Ramsey's "baby steps" to financial recovery helped restore my credit rating to "very good" before the end of my sabbatical. As I got back into the swing of life at work, I was diligent about keeping a monthly spreadsheet of funds coming in and going out. This helped prevent several negative situations from developing. I actually misplaced or didn't receive bills on four or five occasions, and because I had been charting my payments, I was able to see that I hadn't received the bills and pay them online instead, saving myself some late charges

I faced at least one nasty setback financially as a result of my sabbatical. The tax bill for the money I had withdrawn from my Thrift Savings Plan was larger than I had anticipated, because I had forgotten to account for the state tax due. This required me to take out a hefty loan at a high interest rate to pay the tax. Still, even if I had known the correct numbers in the beginning, I would have taken the time off. I'm glad I took the sabbatical, even if it meant robbing my retirement fund.

Troughout the book the names of people from the three-letter agency were changed to protect their identity.

As to my bonus reason for taking a sabbatical—taking care of some unfulfilled dreams—I checked two things off my bucket list: acting in a movie and getting that book about my sabbatical written! I also developed several new interests, one of which was growing plants from seeds. It was so healing to watch small plants turn into flowers and vegetables. I was occasionally frustrated after going back to work with my failure to complete various personal goals I'd laid out, but I still have time to tackle those dreams—including the one about someday owning or working at a retreat center.

Spiritually my sabbatical brought about the most important turning point in my life since salvation. The opportunity to consolidate all that I had learned about the Lord over my lifetime was amazing. To hear from Him, I learned to prioritize time in His Word and in prayer each day. Today I love God more than ever. He is amazing, and I can't wait for all He plans to do with the next chapters in my life.

Sometimes people ask how I manage to remain cheerful during stressful times. Now I don't always remain cheerful, but when I do keep a good attitude, there is a reason: I start each day with time alone in God's Word, and it nourishes my soul. It brings me life. My sabbatical allowed me to slow down time and cultivate this discipline. Not only that, but it gave me the chance to remember the many scars in my past and to relive the subsequent healings. Though I was only off work for five months, it felt as if I'd been in times of refreshing for a year or more.

Investing in myself was worth it. My sabbatical was all about setting aside time for active resting. It was about unburdening myself from as many cares as possible. While my career provided a great way for me to care for the world and love those around me, I needed a window of time to get alone with God and consider what life was really all about. If I hadn't taken time for reflection and rest, I may have looked back with regrets and wondered if I had spent my life in the most profitable way.

My sabbatical was such a beautiful time in my life. Although I'm sure I would have experienced similar times of rest if I had waited until after retirement to slow down, I experienced something so special about calling a timeout from life. While circumstances pushed me toward a sabbatical, I believe it was a divine appointment that I quit my job and made the time to rest.

God took care of me every step of the way. Funds showed up right when I had to have them. Fellowship materialized before I became lonely. The trips I planned taught me great lessons. My return to work came just as resting began to lose its luster.

By all means, plan and take a sabbatical. Do it prayerfully and with your eyes open about the financial consequences. Find a place to rest your mind, find answers to the various hindrances in your life, and come out with a plan to live. A sabbatical of the mind will make you superhuman. It will give you time to explore and appropriate the abundant life that you knew was out there for you.

I leave you with Philippians 4:7–9: "The peace of God, which passeth all understanding, shall keep your hearts and minds through Christ Jesus. Finally, brethren, whatsoever things are true, whatsoever things are honest, whatsoever things are just, whatsoever things are pure, whatsoever things are lovely, whatsoever things are of good report; if there be any virtue, and if there be any praise, think on these things. Those things, which ye have both learned, and received, and heard, and seen in me [Paul], do: and the God of peace shall be with you."

Appendix A

QUESTIONS TO ASK BEFORE AND DURING A SABBATICAL

Before I took my sabbatical, I created a plan. This allowed me to relax into the work of active resting, as I had no need to worry or to be overly concerned about what was coming next. I had the money right, the timing right, and the future right (to the extent that we can ever really count on the future.)

If you are thinking about taking a sabbatical, the considerations I created for myself at the start of my own sabbatical may be of help to you as you begin the process:

1. Begin the sabbatical with a look inward. While it is fresh, write down your thoughts about the work you just left. Include the good, the bad, and the ugly. What did you like about yourself in that job, and what didn't fit your personality? Think about your contributions and how much you did for others to care for the world through your work.

2. Think about the stressors in your life. Work is a magnifier of stress but not the only one. After writing about work stressors, think about other areas that have added tension or pressure to your life. Write down how much and how often you were able to decompress while holding down a job. How did you escape from the routine, and how often were you able to relax and unwind?

3. Where are you physically? Have you pushed certain areas of health to the back burner in the whirlwind of normal life? Have you had a regular physical with a doctor?

4. Prepare to journal about how you feel and react to significant insights during the sabbatical. It is important to learn some lasting lessons during your sabbatical. This will provide a roadmap for your post-sabbatical life. What has to change? What good things should continue into the next phase of life? Is there a lack of fulfillment in your life—something that you sense you should be doing but haven't done yet?

5. If you know you will have to return to regular work after your sabbatical, understand the likely timeline for the reentry process. What are your limitations as to how long you can remain off work? For some this will be money driven. For others, their career may pass them by if they stay away too long. For me, I knew that my money would run out in six to nine months. I also realized that my employers of choice usually took six to twelve weeks to make a selection after a job announcement closed. Therefore I knew I had to start applying for jobs about two months into my sabbatical.

One exercise that I found valuable during my sabbatical was considering the big lessons I'd learned in life before starting the sabbatical. Here are some of the questions I asked myself:

1. What are five to ten of the very best experiences of my life to date? What did I learn from the experiences?

2. What are five to ten of the hardest experiences I've had in my life? What did I learn from the experiences?

3. What kinds of activities, tasks, or projects have given me the most satisfaction?

4. What jobs have I always wanted to do but haven't done? Is it practical to attempt them during or after my sabbatical? (Perhaps I could do them as a volunteer endeavor or as a hobby if not as full-time employment.)

5. What kinds of people interest or excite me? How could I arrange to meet and spend time with these kinds of people? (Think conferences, college courses, online, part-time job, volunteer work.)

6. What has my job experience taught me about my interactions with other people? My church experience?

7. When have I felt the most peaceful as an adult?

8. How successful have I been at handling money? What have I learned about money?

9. What do I enjoy doing the most?

10. What excites me about the future?

11. What would I ask Jesus if I could see Him face to face?

Appendix B

Books I Read on My Sabbatical

Open: An Autobiography by Andre Agassi
Your Money After the Big 5-0 by Larry Burkett
The Complete Guide to Managing Your Money by Larry Burkett
The Scarpetta Factor by Patricia Cornwell

Fear Fighters by Jentezen Franklin
Believe That You Can by Jentezen Franklin
Take Hold of Your Dream by Jentezen Franklin
Small Simple Changes by Rich Kay

King James Bible
The Summer Before the Dark by Doris Lessing
Fearless by Max Lucado
Miracle of Miracles by Mina Nevisa

Going Rogue by Sarah Palin
Financial Peace by Dave Ramsey
Total Money Makeover by Dave Ramsey
Bod 4 God by Steve Reynolds

The Blessed Life by Robert Morris
Walking Miracle by Art Sanborn
The Man Born to Be King by Dorothy L. Sayers
Your Work Matters to God by Doug Sherman and William Hendricks

The Christian's Secret of a Happy Life by Hannah Whitall Smith
The God of All Comfort by Hannah Whitall Smith
Twelve Pillars by Jim Rohn and Chris Widener
The Shack by William Paul Young

Appendix C

FINDING TRUE AND COMPLETE HEALING

God wants each of us to receive all the healing we need. His intent for our healing, however, is that we come to His Son, Jesus. Jesus has the power to forgive our sins and heal every issue in our lives, whether our needs are physical, mental, or spiritual.

Jesus love us, no matter what we've done. He forgave the people who spit on Him, crucified Him, and stood around waiting for Him to die. He can forgive us of anything we've done. We may even have cursed His name, but He won't remember our sin—if we ask Him to forgive us. When we invite Jesus into our hearts to be our Savior, He will never stop loving us. No one or nothing is strong enough to take us out of His hand. He bids us climb into His lap.

Every person born on the earth is born into sin. Babies are not born innocent but with the curse of Adam and Eve on their lives. God doesn't hold them accountable for this sin until they are old enough to reason for themselves, but at some point every person realizes that he is guilty before God and before his fellowman. But there is a cure for this condition—asking Jesus for His forgiveness and His healing.

Jesus Christ, the Savior, defeated all enemies, including the devil, through the finished work of the cross. Jesus was born as human flesh and walked on the earth as part man and part God. He felt emotions just as you and I do. He was beaten and tortured. Then He was hung on a cross until He was dead. After three days sealed in a tomb, He rose from the grave and conquered the final enemy—death. Now those who follow Jesus will also conquer death. Any spiritual warfare that comes to our door cannot end in anything but eventual victory. Even if we die, the moment we pass from this life, we will be ushered into the eternal presence of the Almighty. In essence, we can't lose.

It only takes a minute to ask God for forgiveness and invite Jesus to take control of our lives. He will do it. Write me and tell me if you make this decision. I would love to know about it and to send you a simple booklet. You can contact me through my website at www.sabbaticalofthemind.net.

Notes

Chapter 7: Contemplating a Path to Healing
1. Merriam-Webster, s.v. "Sabbatical," http://www.merriam-webster.com/dictionary/sabbatical (accessed June 9, 2016).

Chapter 12: Facing My Fears
1. Find out more about Steve Reynolds's Losing to Live program and his book Bod 4 God at his website at www.bod4god.org.